The Spectrum Girl's Survival Guide

of related interest

Camouflage
The Hidden Lives of Autistic Women
Dr Sarah Bargiela
Illustrated by Sophie Standing
ISBN 978 1 78592 566 5
eISBN 978 1 78592 667 9

The Asperger Teen's Toolkit
Francis Musgrave
ISBN 978 1 78592 161 2
eISBN 978 1 78450 438 0

The Autism-Friendly Guide to Periods
Robyn Steward
ISBN 978 1 78592 324 1
eISBN 978 1 78450 637 7

Aspergirls
Empowering Females with Asperger Syndrome
Rudy Simone
ISBN 978 1 84905 826 1
eISBN 978 0 85700 289 1

THE SPECTRUM GIRL'S SURVIVAL GUIDE

How to Grow Up Awesome and Autistic

SIENA CASTELLON

Foreword by Temple Grandin

Illustrated by Rebecca Burgess

Jessica Kingsley Publishers
London and Philadelphia

First published in 2020
by Jessica Kingsley Publishers
73 Collier Street
London N1 9BE, UK
and
400 Market Street, Suite 400
Philadelphia, PA 19106, USA

www.jkp.com

Library of Congress Cataloging in Publication Data
A CIP catalog record for this book is available from the Library of Congress

British Library Cataloguing in Publication Data
A CIP catalogue record for this book is available from the British Library

ISBN 978 1 78775 183 5
eISBN 978 1 78775 184 2

Printed and bound in Great Britain

To all the awesome autistic
girls around the world who
dance to a different beat

Contents

Foreword

When I first heard about Siena Castellon, I was really impressed by her positive attitude. She is an accomplished, gifted student in mathematics and physics. Her work makes it very clear the great things that autistic people are capable of. As a high-school student, Siena had completed two prestigious summer programs at the Perimeter Institute for Theoretical Physics in Canada and at the University of Cambridge in Materials Science. She has also been featured in *Materials World Magazine*.

Autism is an important part of who I am, but my career in animal welfare and designing livestock equipment has given me an exciting and meaningful life. The reason I started this foreword describing Siena's mathematical achievements is to show autistic girls that they can be capable of great things. When I talk to both parents and autistic individuals, it is important for them to know that I am a Professor of Animal Science at Colorado State University. This helps motivate both parents and teachers to have high expectations for their autistic children.

During my many lectures on autism, I have many grandfathers and grandmothers come up to me and tell me that they discovered they were on the autism spectrum when their grandchildren were diagnosed. These individuals usually had good careers in engineering, accounting, or sales of specialized commercial equipment.

The book will help you with navigating the social world, but I felt strongly that the reader needed to know some background on the non-autism parts of Siena's life. Do not allow autism to hold you back. What I really like is her positive attitude, because sometimes there is too much negativity. Siena has helped many people have a positive attitude.

Dr. Temple Grandin, author of
Thinking in Pictures and *The Autistic Brain*

Acknowledgments

To all the superhero teachers out there who use their power for good. To the rare few who see the best in us and encourage us to reach for the stars. To Mrs. Mannan and Mrs. Henry who saw my potential and believed in me when others didn't. To Mr. Hall who instilled in me his contagious love of history and Mr. Patterson, my all-time favorite math teacher.

To all my female mentors for their kindness, generosity, support and advice. I am forever grateful. To Imperial College Professor Sara Rankin for her bravery, passion and commitment to neurodiversity. To Dr. Anna Remington, Dr. Laura Crane, Dr. Mel Bovis and Dr. Liz Pellicano (past and present directors and researchers at the Centre for Research in Autism and Education (CRAE)) for giving me my first work placement and my first research paper opportunity, and for empowering me to see my autism as a strength. To Dr. Jessica Wade for teaching me the power of sisterhood.

To Anna Kennedy OBE, the founder of autism charity Anna Kennedy Online, Dr. Tony Lloyd, the CEO of the ADHD Foundation, and Tania Tirraoro, founder of Special Needs Jungle, for their guidance, wisdom and whole-hearted belief in me and Neurodiversity Celebration Week.

To my family: my dad, my mom and my sister for all their love, encouragement, belief and sacrifice. For all the battles that we've fought and all the victories we've had. A special thank you to my mom, who shares in all my joys and sorrows, for her infinite love, dedication and devotion. Thank you for never letting an injustice go unchallenged and for teaching me that the best view comes after the hardest climb. I hope that every autistic teen girl has someone like you in their corner.

To my awesome dog, Rico, for his unconditional love during the best of times and the worst of times.

To Jessica Kingsley Publishers and Andrew James for giving me an opportunity to reach out to my autistic sisters. I hope I can make their journey less bumpy than mine.

Finally, a million thank-yous to the two remarkable autistic women who contributed to this book. Your encouragement and support have meant the world to me. Thank you to Dr. Temple Grandin for being a trailblazer and an inspiration, and for writing the foreword to this book, and to the talented Rebecca Burgess for her amazing illustrations and comics.

Oh...and thank you to the many bullies who tried to break me. In an odd twist of fate, I have you to thank for finding my voice and motivating me to share my story.

About Me

I'm 16 years old. In many ways, I'm a typical teenage girl. I love music, binge-watching TV shows on Netflix, makeup, chocolate and my awesome dog, Rico. Yet there is one important thing about me that makes me very different from most teenage girls. I'm autistic. I'm also dyslexic and dyspraxic, and I have ADHD (attention deficit hyperactivity disorder).

If you're reading this book, chances are that you're autistic too. I wrote this book especially for you. Although lots of books have been written about autism and Asperger's syndrome, most have been written by people who aren't autistic (**neurotypicals**) or by autistic adults who are a long way from their childhood. I'm writing this book because I would've really benefited from a book that was specifically written for autistic teen girls by another autistic teen girl. A practical and informative book written by someone like you: someone who knows and understands what it's like to be an autistic teen girl in the digital age of Snapchat, Instagram, WhatsApp, YouTube and selfies. I hope you find this book helpful.

I'm a shy and soft-spoken person by nature, which makes me an unlikely candidate to write this book.

However, one thing I've learned is that life rarely goes as planned and that sometimes you can find yourself on a very unexpected journey.

When I was 13, I designed and created www.qlmentoring.com, a website to support and mentor autistic students and students with learning differences. When researching my various conditions online, I discovered that the information and resources were targeted at parents. I found it odd that I was unable to find information or resources written especially for me. I decided to change this by creating a site where young people could go to get practical advice on how to overcome some of the challenges caused by having special educational needs. On my website, I share the tips and tricks I use to succeed in school, and I provide advice on what to do if you're being bullied.

As a natural progression from my website, I joined Twitter and Instagram (@QLMentoring and @NCWeek) and began sharing my thoughts about autism, special educational needs and the education system. Although I didn't set out to do so, I gradually became a neurodiversity advocate and an anti-bullying campaigner. I began to use my voice to share my experiences and to try to change negative perceptions and stereotypes about autism and learning differences.

Before I knew it, I was winning lots of national awards, including the Points of Light award from Prime Minister Theresa May in August 2018 and the prestigious Diana Award in September 2018. I also received the British Citizen Youth Award and was invited to a small reception to meet the Duke and Duchess of Cambridge at Kensington Palace in October 2018. By far the most surreal experience was winning the 2018 BBC Radio 1 Teen Hero Award! A BBC film crew came to my home to make a short film about me. The film was played at Wembley Arena shortly before I appeared on stage to collect my award in front of 10,000 teens. As part of my Teen Hero Award surprise, Lana Del Rey (my absolute favorite musician of all time) and the awesome Shawn Mendes sent me personalized videos congratulating me. I also went on a private tour of the Harry Potter Studios, received a Harry Potter book signed by the legendary J.K. Rowling and met the incredible Callum Turner (he plays Newt's younger brother Theseus in the movie *Fantastic Beasts: The Crimes of Grindelwald*). Callum even invited me to the London premiere.

As I said earlier, sometimes you can find yourself on a very unexpected journey. I would certainly never have predicted that my humble website and autism advocacy would end up catapulting me into chilling backstage with Little Mix and giving an acceptance speech on live TV to the millions of viewers across the United Kingdom watching the Teen Hero Awards. I don't think that the dozens of people who have mercilessly bullied me over the years would have predicted it either.

Having said that, my most satisfying moments are those outside the limelight. Those quiet, unexpected moments that come after a long day at school. The email from a teenage girl thanking me because she was diagnosed with dyspraxia and autism as a result of reading the information on my website. The email from a ten-year-old boy letting me know that my bullying advice helped him and sharing that he recently won a prize for his creative writing. I treasure those moments the most. Knowing that each of us has the power to make a positive difference to someone's life is what led me to write this book.

I hope that this book reminds you that you're not alone. Being an autistic teen girl can be lonely and isolating. I want you to know that there are many of us out there. With each passing day, we are coming out of the shadows and embracing who we are. Never be ashamed of being different: it is this difference that makes you extraordinary and unique. I view my autism as a strength and as an advantage, a modern-day superpower. Our brains are wired differently, which means we see and perceive the world differently. Where others may see limitations, we see possibilities. We are the innovators, the problem-solvers, the pioneers, the visionaries and the trailblazers of tomorrow. We have the potential to make significant contributions to society. So never stop believing that you have the potential to be exceptional. I certainly won't. As far as I am concerned, you're amazing and I'm thrilled to be part of your journey.

2

The Invisible Autistic Girl

Unfortunately, there are still lots of stereotypes and misconceptions about autism, especially in relation to autism in girls. When I tell people that I'm autistic, they frequently express disbelief. I'm often told that I don't look autistic or act like someone who is autistic. I've even had well-meaning people try to compliment me by telling me that I look "normal" and am great at "fooling" people. I still haven't come up with the ideal response, in particular because these comments imply that there is something wrong with being autistic. Let me be very clear: I like being autistic. Autism is an integral part of who I am. It's not something that I'm ashamed of. On the contrary, I embrace my autism because my autism and learning differences make me *me*.

To my classmates, teachers and acquaintances, I can appear conventionally normal. I can make friends and be sociable. I'm well behaved, intelligent and have a sense of humor. In their eyes, I don't exhibit the behaviors commonly associated with autism. I appear to make eye contact (I actually look at people's foreheads). I don't have meltdowns or hit myself or others, and I don't drone on and on about esoteric interests. I defy their understanding of what autism is and what autism

21

looks like. However, as you and I know, appearances can be deceiving.

Despite outward appearances, inside we're very different. I've always known I was different—like an alien from a different planet. It's very likely that you have always felt different too. Social interaction doesn't come naturally to me. Whereas other children automatically developed and absorbed social skills while frolicking in the playground, I studied people the way others might study a foreign language. Without knowing it, I became a social anthropologist and an actress. I studied social norms and rules, I mimicked behavior and scripted conversations so as to appear "normal" and to fit in. Yet, no matter how hard I tried, I couldn't avoid making embarrassing social blunders. I always felt that I was on the outside looking in.

Although I have always known that I was different, I didn't know why. To be honest, it never occurred to me that I could be autistic. I too fell into the trap of thinking of autism in the rigid one-dimensional way it's depicted in the media. Before I was diagnosed, I viewed autism as the stereotypical boy sprawled on the supermarket floor covering his ears and screaming during a meltdown, or as the eccentric boy who could memorize thousands of train schedules but was unable to have a conversation. At the time, I didn't know that autism is a spectrum disorder. I didn't know that there's a huge range within the autism spectrum that spans from severely autistic to mildly autistic, and that where you fall on the spectrum constantly changes. I also thought it mostly affected boys.

I was diagnosed as being autistic when I was 12. I count myself lucky to have been diagnosed at a relatively young age because I have met lots of women who weren't diagnosed until well into their 40s and 50s. Imagine living your entire adult life knowing you are different, but not knowing why. My diagnosis was welcome. I had spent my entire school life being rejected and ostracized by my classmates, and I was beginning to believe that I was unlikeable. My autism diagnosis finally gave me the answer as to why I'm different. I was no longer shy, timid and eccentric or, worse, weird and odd. I was autistic. Autism, a six-letter word, explained *everything*. It explained my aversion to loud sounds and bright lights, my sensitivity to smells and touch, and my intolerance of labels, seams and certain fabrics. It explained my advanced vocabulary, my adult sense of humor and my encyclopedic knowledge of dinosaurs when I was four and Harry Potter when I was seven. It explained my aptitude for mathematics and physics. It explained why I find social interaction challenging and why I was frequently bullied. It explained my stomach problems, my food intolerances and my insomnia. It explained my social anxiety. It was like finally finding the elusive missing piece of a jigsaw puzzle. My life finally made sense.

Another benefit of finding out that I'm autistic is that I stopped feeling isolated and alone. I took great comfort from knowing that there are other people out there who are just like me. People who understand me and accept me for who I am. Since my diagnosis, I've been fortunate to meet many amazing autistic people. Whatever our differences, we're kindred spirits. We share a special connection, a bond forged from knowing that no one else can truly understand what it's like to be autistic.

As soon as I was diagnosed as autistic, I began to research autism. I scoured the Internet for information and read books, articles, blogs and studies on autism. What I learned was a revelation. I learned that the little I had previously known about autism was wrong, especially in relation to autism in girls. For the first time, I realized that my social communication difficulties, my sensory sensitivities, my anxiety, my insomnia, my stomach problems and my poor coordination were *interconnected*. I also realized that not everyone perceives and experiences the world as I do. For example, I learned that not everyone sees numbers the way I do. To me, numbers have personalities. Each has a color and smell. I can visually flip, rotate and shuffle them. This is a condition called synesthesia, which is common in people who are autistic.

I also learned that one of the reasons girls are less likely to be diagnosed as autistic is that we're really good at hiding our autistic traits. In fact, we become so good at pretending to be "normal" that we convince everyone that we're neurotypical. Eventually, the constant pretense and heightened state of anxiety becomes too much for us to cope with. This can have a negative effect on our mental health. Some of us develop eating disorders or obsessive compulsive disorder (OCD), some of us begin to self-harm and many of us become depressed. It is usually at this stage, when we have hit rock bottom and are crying out for help, that people start to put the pieces together and that our autism, which has been hiding in plain sight, is finally recognized.

Not everyone embraces their autism as quickly as I did. For some autistic girls, it's more of a journey. The idea of being different can be scary and overwhelming. It can also feel unfair. You may wish that you could be like everyone else. You're absolutely entitled to feel that way. I've felt that way at times too, especially when my sensory sensitivities are wreaking havoc on me or when I'm being bullied. If you're still struggling to come to terms with being autistic, I hope that this book helps you to see that you're no longer alone. You're part of a tribe who know what you've been through and who see you and accept you for who you are.

3

Embracing Who You Are

When I was diagnosed as being autistic, it came as welcome news. I finally had an explanation for why I struggle with social interaction and have sensory overloads. It's a huge relief to know that my brain is just wired differently, which is why I find some things harder than neurotypicals and find some things easier than neurotypicals.

Having a label placed on you can be scary. From one day to the next, people start using labels like "autistic," "high-functioning," "Asperger's syndrome" and "disabled" to describe you. It can feel as if your autism diagnosis is swallowing you and that your past self no longer exists. Another concern you may have about finding out that you're autistic is that people may not respond well to the news, especially since there's still a stigma and lots of misconceptions about what it means to be autistic. So how do you reconcile the peace of mind that comes from knowing why you're different with the drawbacks of having a label placed on you that carries a lot of baggage?

VIEWING AUTISTIC STRENGTHS AS A SUPERPOWER

Knowing that you're biologically "different" can be confusing. Society places a lot of importance on people being the same. I'm a huge fan of the *X-Men* movies because I identify with them. The storylines have lots of parallels with how the autism community is treated. The X-Men are misfits and outcasts who fight to save a world that fears them. Their mutation is both a blessing and a curse. The superpowers that they repeatedly use to save the world are the reason they're rejected and vilified.

"Autism" is a loaded word. Some people are scared of it. Others may think less of you. At school, I've been called a "freak" and a "weirdo." I have been treated unkindly and have been bullied. In the same way that the X-Men are feared and looked down upon because of their superpowers, we are feared and looked down upon for our autism. The media often makes the problem worse by depicting autism as a scary disease that needs to be cured. The deep-seated stereotypes and the negative way in which the media portrays autism can make it difficult to accept your autism.

It's really important to stand your ground and to not get swept away by how others want to define and perceive you. One of the benefits of being autistic is that we have many strengths, which I prefer to call superpowers. Here is a list of some of our superpowers:

- We're honest.

- We have a strong sense of fairness and justice.

- We're loyal and trustworthy.

- We're sincere.

- We're not judgmental.

- We're accepting of people who are different.

- We're kind.

- We're dependable.

- We're conscientious.

- We're creative.

- We think outside the box.

- We're level-headed.

- We have an unconventional sense of humor.

- We're logical.

- We're analytical.

- We're problem-solvers.

- We're great at entertaining ourselves.

- We love learning.

- We're focused and persistent.

These are amazing qualities that make me proud to be autistic.

UNDERSTANDING YOUR AUTISTIC BRAIN

When people say that autistic brains are wired differently, they mean that an autistic brain differs from that of a neurotypical brain. There is an implication that because our brain deviates from the norm (the neurotypical brain), our brain is somehow faulty or inferior. What if this isn't true? What if nature designed the two brains to be different for a reason?

The neurotypical brain is optimally designed to facilitate socialization. It allows neurotypicals to interact socially and communicate with ease. It gives neurotypicals the ability to read body language, understand facial expressions and subtle fluctuations in tone of voice, understand different points of view, hidden messages, innuendo and other forms of communication. On the other hand, the autistic brain is optimally designed to focus on the physical world in much greater detail, to recognize patterns and shapes, to be logical, analytical and focused, to develop areas of expertise and to focus on understanding the world around us.

Although these two brains serve different purposes, they complement each other. Neither is better or worse. The neurotypical brain is designed to facilitate the development of communities and civilizations and to collectively coordinate human behavior, whereas the autistic brain is designed to allow us to analyze and systemize, and to discern details and patterns that enable human beings to understand how the world around us works. This knowledge has been used to advance the development of society. Some of the world's most famous scientists are thought to have been autistic—scientists such as Albert Einstein, Charles Darwin and Sir Isaac Newton.

WHEN LABELS ARE PROBLEMATIC

You may find that some people like to divide autistic individuals into two categories: high-functioning and low-functioning. The two categories allow neurotypicals to separate us into autistic individuals who appear to be normal and autistic individuals who are very obviously severely autistic and require round-the-clock care. I really dislike it when people do this. When neurotypicals learn that I'm autistic, a typical response is that I must be really high-functioning. I'm complimented for appearing "normal." It's as if they're saying that I'm only a little bit autistic. This underhanded compliment implies that I'm lucky because I can pass off as neurotypical. It also implies that since I'm less visibly autistic, I must have a mild, diluted form of autism that is imperceptible and therefore can only have a minimal effect on my life.

There is no easy form of autism. Being autistic in a neurotypical world is hard. Being an autistic teen girl is even harder. Trying to make sense of all the senseless social mind games that teens play is hard. Trying to figure out what to say and what not to say, what to wear and what not to wear, and what to like and what not to like, so that you don't end up being ostracized and bullied by your classmates, is hard. Being in constant discomfort or pain caused by sensory processing issues and enduring it in silence is hard. Dealing with crippling social anxiety is hard. Constantly pretending to be someone you're not, in order to try to fit in, is hard. Just because many of our challenges are invisible and we use all our willpower to maintain our composure doesn't mean that we have a lesser form of autism. Autism is autism; you are either autistic or you're not.

I also object to the way that so-called "low-functioning" autistic individuals are written off. These individuals may be non-verbal and may need 24/7 care, but that doesn't mean they are any less intelligent or awesome. It just means they need more support. The "low-functioning" label ignores strengths, whereas the "high-functioning" label ignores weaknesses. Both are damaging. Levels of functioning can also change over a period of time. There are lots of autistic adults who were once labeled as low-functioning because they were non-verbal as children. Labeling someone as low-functioning can result in other people lowering their expectations of what the person can learn and achieve. Professor Temple Grandin was once thought to be unteachable. She eventually went to university and is now an author and a world-famous professor of animal science.

Another objection I have about the use of the "high-functioning" and "low-functioning" labels is that they imply that the degree to which we can function is static—that it stays the same. You and I know that this isn't true. We have good days and bad days. On a bad day, I qualify as being low-functioning and non-verbal. For example, there have been times when I've had a miserable day at school. If I'm bullied at school, my anxiety will skyrocket. Since my anxiety levels and sensory processing issues are interlinked, I'll have a tough time enduring the usual crowds, loud noises and fluorescent lights. I'll be in a state of constant pain. By the time I leave school, I'll barely be keeping it together. I may even reach the point where I have an autistic shutdown, which means I'll be unable to communicate, interact or socialize. All I'll want is to go somewhere quiet and still, so that I can recover. I suspect you've had similar experiences.

TO TELL OR NOT TO TELL

Just because you have been diagnosed as autistic doesn't mean you have to tell anyone. There is no right or wrong answer as to whether you should tell others that you're autistic. It is a very personal decision. There are benefits and drawbacks to disclosing that you're autistic. It's important to consider all the pros and cons because once you tell people, you can't take it back.

There are lots of benefits to disclosing your autism. Below are some of the benefits:

- **It makes it much easier to get the help and support you need.** One of the main benefits of letting others know you're autistic is that it helps others to be more supportive of your specific needs, especially in relation to your sensory sensitivities and any communication difficulties you may have.

- **It gives you the freedom to be yourself.** Many autistic teen girls are afraid that their classmates will judge them for being different and so try hard to pretend to be like everyone else. Pretending to be someone you're not is exhausting. Being free to be yourself can take a huge weight off your shoulders.

- **It allows others to understand you.** Since autism is an invisible condition, we are often misunderstood. Sometimes other people view our actions and behavior as strange or perceive us as being difficult. If others know you're autistic, they will be able to understand why you may sometimes react and behave differently to other teens. The more open you are about your autism and how your autism affects you, the better prepared people will be to help and support you.

- **It helps to educate others about autism.** Telling people that you're autistic not only helps you, but also helps other autistic people. If more autistic people are open about being autistic, it will help to change people's perceptions and stereotypes about autism. The more neurotypicals learn about autism, the more understanding and supportive they can be towards the autism community.

Some autistic individuals choose to keep their autism diagnosis private. Below are some of the drawbacks of telling people that you're autistic:

- **People may treat you differently.** You may be concerned that others will treat you differently or view you differently. If you're a private person, you may not want to draw any unnecessary attention to yourself. You also can't predict how someone will react. Sharing your diagnosis may make some people uncomfortable. It may even cause them to avoid you.

- **People may not understand autism.** Most people don't understand autism as well as they should. They don't know what it's like to be autistic. There are also still many stereotypes and misconceptions about what autism is. In fact, some people still think that girls can't be autistic.

Since I am proud of being autistic, I am generally open about it. However, there have been a few times when I have regretted confiding in someone. For example, last summer I spent two weeks at Perimeter Institute's summer program in Canada, a theoretical physics program for young physicists. (Did I mention that I'm a math and physics nerd?) On a five-hour bus ride to tour a dark matter research lab, I sat next to a boy who was really friendly. We chatted most of the way to the lab and most of the way back. Since we had a lot in common, I got the impression that we would become friends. A few miles before the end of our journey back to our dorm, I mentioned that I'm an autism advocate and that I'm passionate about changing negative perceptions of autism. His demeanor immediately changed. We never spoke again. For the remainder of the summer program, he avoided me. It was as if he thought I had some infectious disease. This is not the only time I have been rejected because someone has a prejudice against autistic individuals. It has happened a few times. You can take the view that how the person treated you says more about them than it does about you. A person who is judgmental and intolerant of people who are different is unlikely to be a good friend. But no matter which way you look at it, it's still hurtful and disappointing.

TELLING FAMILY MEMBERS

You'd think that family members would be especially understanding and supportive about learning that you're autistic. If only life were that simple! Unfortunately, even family members can be judgmental and close-minded, especially if they are older and have antiquated views on what it means to be "normal."

When deciding whether to disclose to a family member, I suggest that you take two factors into consideration. First, whether it would be beneficial to you for them to know. If you spend a lot of time with them, it may be important for them to know. Second, whether you think they will be open-minded and accepting. If the family member is going to focus on trying to cure you of autism or be ashamed of you, I wouldn't tell them.

For the most part, I think relatives are supportive. Since autism runs in families, it is very likely that your family has other members who are autistic. After I was diagnosed, I realized that I had an aunt, an uncle and possibly a grandfather who are undiagnosed autistics. Although my younger sister has not been officially diagnosed, we think she's autistic too. So I'm by no means the only autistic person in my family and it's very unlikely that you are too.

TELLING YOUR SCHOOL

I strongly recommend that you tell your school. Although I have been shocked by how little some school staff at mainstream schools know about autism, I have found that disclosing my autism has helped. Before I was diagnosed as autistic, I was always getting judged for not being more social and for not participating more in class. My teachers would sometimes jump to conclusions to explain some of my behaviors. For example, one of the few times I got reprimanded was for small uniform infractions. One teacher in particular was obsessed with making sure that I had the top button of my shirt fastened. The problem was that the shirt was scratchy and rough and rubbed against my skin. The discomfort was so distracting that I had a hard time concentrating in my lessons. So I unfastened the top button—not to be rebellious or as a fashion statement, but to relieve my sensory sensitivities so that I could focus on my schoolwork. Unfortunately, this one teacher was relentless about enforcing the uniform code and so I was always getting in trouble for having my top button undone. After I was diagnosed and I explained my sensory processing issues, my school became more flexible with the uniform code.

I vividly recall one experience where my autism diagnosis would have come in really handy. I was at a small mainstream school with only six people in my class. We were in the last year of the school, before moving on to secondary school. I was ten. That year our drama teacher chose *The Jungle Book* to be the end-of-year school play. Our class was given the biggest roles—it was our swan song, our final performance at the school. For the avoidance of doubt, I am a dreadful stage actress! Much to my dismay, I was given the role of Bagheera, the black panther. The role involved wearing a black furry onesie with a hood, while prowling around the stage like a cat under beaming spotlights that generated more heat than the sun. It was torture! The furry onesie was so blazingly hot and itchy. It felt as if I was being roasted alive, while thousands of insects were crawling and burrowing beneath my skin. I tried to explain my distress to the drama teacher, but she insisted that playing the part would be good for me. I was even accused of being melodramatic and of being a diva. Needless to say, I was a dreadful Bagheera. I was too focused on my sensory pain and discomfort to put my heart and soul into my performance. A week before the performance, the headmistress called my mom to tell her that I wasn't taking the play seriously and was going to ruin the production for everyone. My mom was told that either I had to drastically improve my performance or I would be excluded from the play. I ended up persevering, but what was supposed to have been a fun experience became a really traumatic one. I wasn't deliberately setting out to ruin the play; in reality, I was making an enormous effort despite being in a lot of pain and discomfort. I'd like to think that if my school had known I was autistic, they would have listened to me and been less judgmental and quick to think the worst of me.

TELLING YOUR CLASSMATES

Telling your classmates that you're autistic can be daunting and frightening. For one thing, you really don't know how they're going to react. It could be that your classmates are really accepting, understanding and supportive. Knowing that you're autistic may help them to understand you better and to clarify any misunderstandings that they may have had about the way you sometimes act or respond to certain situations. On the other hand, your classmates could react negatively and use your autism as another reason to tease or bully you.

One autistic girl I know (whom I will refer to as Leslie) gets very distressed when she is unable to sit in the same seat that she always sits in at lunchtime. Although she tried to explain this to her friends, they felt Leslie was being unreasonable and that one seat was as good as any other. Even Leslie struggled to make sense of why being unable to sit in her usual seat caused her to become so anxious, unsettled and upset. In fact, Leslie found that she was unable to stop fixating on it for the rest of the day. It wasn't until Leslie was diagnosed as being autistic that she realized that sticking to a routine (in this case, sitting in the same seat) is a characteristic of autism. When she explained this to her friends, they were able to understand why sitting in the same seat was important to Leslie. It helped them to know that Leslie has difficulty adjusting to a sudden change in her routine.

A drawback of telling your classmates that you're autistic is that it can make you an easy target for teasing and bullying. Sadly, some kids aren't very nice.

There will always be mean kids who will take advantage of classmates whom they perceive as vulnerable and an easy target. We've all met them. The kid who likes building himself or herself up by putting others down. The class bully who takes pleasure from causing misery and from abusing and traumatizing others. These types of kids are likely to use your autism as ammunition against you. In all likelihood, these kids have already been unkind to you. They're the type of person who will call you derogatory names and who will circulate gossip and false rumors. I'd like to be able to say that your other classmates will stand up for you if they witness you being mistreated. Unfortunately, I know from experience that most bystanders don't get involved; instead, they look the other way. If you believe that telling your classmates that you're autistic will make life more difficult for you at school, then don't tell them.

STRENGTH IN NUMBERS

I find it really liberating to be around other autistic girls. One of the many benefits of being friends with another autistic girl is that you can remove your mask and be yourself without fear of being judged or misunderstood. You can also be honest and open with each other about the difficulties and challenges of being autistic. We speak the same language. We share the same experience. We get each other in a way that neurotypicals never will.

Unfortunately, I rarely meet other autistic girls. A few months ago, I met a 16-year-old autistic girl who had never met another autistic girl. It may be that you're friends with lots of autistic girls. But it's more likely that you don't know many other autistic girls, especially if you go to a mainstream school. I think it's important to our self-identity and self-esteem to spend time with girls who are like us.

One way of doing this is by joining a local social group for autistic girls. One may already exist. You or your parents may want to call some local autism charities to find out if there any local groups in your area. If one doesn't exist and you think you could benefit from joining or creating a local autistic girls' social group, ask your parents to help. It's easy to start a group on Facebook and to advertise on social media platforms such as Twitter. I recently visited a group of tween autistic girls in Croydon in south London. One of their parents reached out to me on Twitter. It was refreshing and liberating to spend time with girls like me. I find it fascinating to talk to autistic girls who have different intense interests to mine. You can learn a lot of fascinating information from them. Best of all, it's liberating to be around girls who see the real me and who accept me for who I am. You deserve to be seen and accepted for who you are too.

4

The Importance of Being Yourself

We're often told that it's important to be yourself. Social media is overflowing with inspirational quotes about embracing who you are and being true to yourself. However, this is much easier said than done. It's hard to be yourself in a world that's determined to turn you into everyone else. Being true to yourself means not worrying about pleasing other people and not living by other people's standards and expectations. Yet society teaches us that conformity is the easiest path to follow. We're under constant pressure to be like everyone else. The truth is that people who are different are often treated harshly.

MASKING TO FIT IN

Most people want to be accepted. Autistic girls are no exception. Some people fit in effortlessly, whereas others find it more difficult. Unfortunately, autistic girls are at a disadvantage because we don't understand social cues, and our classmates often perceive our autistic behavior and intense interests as strange. Many of us realize that the best way to be accepted and to avoid being judged and rejected by others is to act like everyone else—to alter our behavior and edit our personality so others will like us. This requires most autistic girls to mask. **Masking** is when we try to hide being autistic so that others will accept us. We suppress our autism so that we can try to behave in a way that neurotypicals will like or will think is "normal" and socially acceptable. Sometimes autistic people also use the term "passing" or "camouflaging." Whichever term we use, many of us feel compelled to conceal our social difficulties and sensory sensitivities so that we aren't punished or made to suffer for being autistic.

Some examples of masking behaviors include:

- observing and copying other people's behavior

- forcing ourselves to make eye contact

- forcing ourselves to vary our facial expressions

- using body language that matches the body language of the person we're interacting with

- preparing and memorizing a script for possible routes a social conversation could take

- forcing ourselves to hide our sensory sensitivities, such as our sensitivity to sound, lights and touch

- refraining from stemming and from discussing our intense interests

- assuming the identity and interests of someone we think neurotypicals will like.

Nearly everyone makes small concessions to fit in better or to act in accordance with social rules and expectations, but the difference is that autistic masking requires constant and elaborate effort. We're always trying to decipher social rules and norms that most of us find bewildering, especially since many are illogical and contradictory. One of the unspoken social rules I struggle with is society's expectation that we tell white lies. Although we're told it is wrong to lie, we quickly learn that there are instances when lying is not only permitted but expected. For example, if someone asks you if you like their new haircut, it isn't socially acceptable to say that you hate it, even if you genuinely feel that way. Instead, you're expected to lie in order to spare someone's feelings. You're expected to say the opposite of what you think.

Since social rules and norms do not come naturally to us, many of us figure out how we're "supposed" to act by observing and imitating those around us, and from watching TV shows and movies. Many autistic girls develop a repertoire of personas that they assume for different situations and audiences. We become performers. I watch different types of TV shows to study the behavior of a particular group of people, to learn their body language, facial expressions, gestures, mannerisms, figures of speech and phrases.

When I was younger, I used to adapt my personality and behavior to blend in. Although I felt different to the other girls in my school, I didn't want to appear *too* different. I tried my best to fit in. I prepared and memorized scripts for social conversations. I studied the girls I wanted to be friends with. I pretended to be interested in whatever interested them. Since they were avid fans of One Direction, I feigned an interest in the band, even though I didn't like their music. I resolved to keep my intense interests to myself, in case I bored the other girls. I bent over backwards to be easy-going and agreeable, determined never to upset or disappoint them. I developed a few friendships, but they were never true friendships. I was playing a part. I was always aware that the friendships were not genuine because I never allowed my friends to meet the real me. I have learned that it is impossible to build an authentic and meaningful friendship on a foundation of deception and pretense.

SOCIAL EXHAUSTION

Pretending to be someone that you're not is exhausting and stressful. We often live in fear of unknowingly saying or doing the wrong thing. We also live in fear of being exposed as imposters. Whenever I have a social conversation with someone, I am simultaneously having an inner dialogue in my head. Am I talking too much? Should I vary my facial expression? Am I using appropriate body language? Should I speak now? Did I say the wrong thing? What do I say next? I'm in a constant state of panic and alertness, afraid of misinterpreting or missing a social cue.

Walking this emotional tightrope can lead to social exhaustion. It takes a lot of energy to play a role in order to get through the school day. Many autistic girls cope with social exhaustion by behaving very differently at home and at school. At school, we use all our energy to suppress our autistic traits. We're often seen as well-behaved, model students. However, it's exhausting trying to impress your teachers, interact with your classmates, stifle the pain and discomfort from your sensory sensitivities and manage your anxiety, all while trying to fit in and do well in your classes. By the time we get home, we're overwhelmed by the tension and distress that we've been bottling up all day.

It may be that by the time you get home you're frazzled. You may feel as if you're ready to explode. You may have a meltdown, start an argument, be belligerent or generally act out. Your parents may find this very confusing. They may be baffled by how differently you behave in school and at home. It's as if you're two different people, which in some ways you are. At school you're concealing your autism, whereas at home it's safe to be yourself. You know that your parents will still love you. It's not that you're deliberately being difficult or trying to get attention. You've been holding in all your anxiety and emotions that have been building up at school all day, waiting to release them in an environment where you feel safe.

If you find that you're lashing out when you get home, I suggest that you tell your family how you're feeling. Consider asking them to read this chapter. Tell them that after a long day at school you need time to yourself to recover and recharge. When you get home from school, do something that you find relaxing and that will help you to unwind. Take a bath or a nap. Go for a walk. Listen to music. Read a book. Bake a cake. Whatever the activity may be, do something soothing and calming that works for you. My family knows that as soon as I get home from a long day at school, I need an hour to myself to decompress and recover. I go to my room and listen to music, play with my dog, read or watch some TV. I need this time to myself. It's very likely that you need some time to yourself too.

LOSS OF IDENTITY

When I was younger, there were times when I was unable to distinguish between the real me and the many characters and roles I played. I often became whoever I spent the most time around, to the point that I even picked up their accent and mannerisms. I often became a carbon copy of the people around me.

A major drawback of pretending to be someone else and playing so many different roles is that it's easy to lose sight of our true identity. We're like chameleons who change their color to match their environment. We become experts at disappearing into the background. Eventually, we get muddled and confused about who we are.

Pretending to be someone else is damaging to our self-esteem and sense of self-worth. Many of us are forced to mask because we believe that we won't be accepted and embraced for who we are. This implies that there is something wrong with us, that we're somehow damaged and unworthy. It also implies that we don't feel safe to be ourselves. We wouldn't feel this way if society made more effort to understand and to accept people who are autistic. It's sad that society still has a long way to go before it accepts people who are different. I take comfort in knowing that we're not the first marginalized group to feel pressured to hide their true identity for fear of recrimination or judgment.

It wasn't long ago that the LGBTQ community was in our shoes. Look how far they have come.

WHEN MASKING BACKFIRES

Although we mask in order to fit in, sometimes it can backfire and have the opposite effect. Social interaction is complicated. It doesn't always lend itself to imitation. For example, when I was much younger, a boy in my class made a joke and everybody laughed. I desperately wanted to make my classmates laugh too. I memorized the joke and repeated it to the same classmates on more than one occasion, hoping to get the same response. I didn't. Instead of laughing, my classmates were irritated and annoyed. At the time, I found this confusing. I now know that there were delicate, unspoken social nuances and rules in play that I was unaware of. At the time, I didn't know that most jokes are only funny the first time you hear them and that it's fine to repeat a joke, as long as you tell it to a different group of people. The older you get and the more you study social interaction, the better you will become at identifying and following unspoken social nuances and rules.

An unintended consequence of masking is that, if taken to an extreme, copying other people can come across as creepy. Most teen girls observe and follow trends in clothing, makeup and hairstyles, and copy them. This is true of autistic girls too. The difference is that some of us may be more literal in the way that we copy trends and behaviors. We may latch on to the most popular girl in our class and meticulously copy the way she acts, looks and dresses in the hope that doing so will help us to fit in. It may be that the girl wears her hair in an elaborate braid and has a whale-shaped pencil case and a purple backpack. So you start wearing your hair the same way and buy an identical pencil case and backpack. It is likely that your attempt to imitate the girl in the hope of replicating her popularity will have the opposite effect. She may get upset with you for stealing her unique look, and your classmates may think you have an unhealthy obsession with her. The trick is to strike the right balance between blending in and maintaining your own identity. If you show up to school looking like a clone of a classmate, you've taken things a bit too far.

At school, autistic girls are often made to feel bad about themselves. Our classmates often focus on our differences, rather than on our many positive qualities. Autistic girls have some amazing qualities and make great friends. We're fiercely loyal and straightforward. We're honest. We've got a great sense of humor. We stand up for others. We're reliable and accepting. We're forgiving. We're interesting and conscientious. We're kind. No matter what your classmates tell you and no matter how they treat you, never be ashamed of being autistic. One of the reasons that I'm writing this book is that I hope it will help you to see how amazing you are. I hope that you'll hold your head high and be proud to be autistic.

MASKING AND MENTAL HEALTH

Masking is mentally, physically and emotionally draining. It takes a lot of effort, self-control and concentration. A combination of the effort it takes to mask and the sense of loss of identity can eventually affect your mental health and lead to severe anxiety and depression. Autistic people call this **social burnout**.

If you're feeling overwhelmed and are having a difficult time coping, it's important to tell your parents, a teacher or someone you trust so that they can help you and get you the support you need. Suffering in silence only makes things worse. Social burnout is very common in people who are autistic, so you're definitely not alone. As soon as you tell someone how you're feeling, you'll feel a sense of relief. I know that it can feel scary to ask for help. The first step is always the hardest. But I know you can do it. Remember that your family love you and want the best for you. I believe in you and want the best for you too.

BEING YOURSELF

Masking is our way of trying to survive in a neurotypical world. Somewhere along the way, we learned that being autistic is not socially acceptable. We're often criticized, judged, rejected and bullied. We learn that the best way to avoid negative attention and to feel safe is to pretend to be like everyone else.

However, we're not like everyone else. Since our disability is invisible, and we suffer in silence, most people do not understand the obstacles we face on a daily and hourly basis. To me, stepping out into the world is a Herculean task that takes courage and resolve. I have to defeat a sensory overload of noise, lights, smells and touch, and I have to battle against my social anxiety, an anxiety that comes from being afraid of saying or doing the wrong thing.

On an ordinary day, as I head out to school, my senses are assaulted as soon as I open my front door. The sounds of cars, motorcycles and construction work reverberate with a deafening noise. On the subway, people push past me, their perfumes, shaving cream, scented lotions, floral deodorants and morning coffee mixing into a sickly, overwhelming smell that makes me queasy. I begin to feel faint. As people inadvertently brush past me, the place I'm touched begins to throb. Before long, my whole body is throbbing. I try not to focus on the pulsating pain and the noxious smells and the cacophony of noise and the flickering lights glaring at me.

As I walk towards school, I try to shut out the world. I try to block the shrieking sirens, the toxic fumes and smell of rotting trash that's patiently waiting on the sidewalk for collection. I struggle to carry my school bag as it gets heavier and heavier with each step. My vision begins to blur. I focus on walking without tripping. I listen to soothing music as a distraction. I take deep breaths. I think of cuddling my dog. Yet my heart is racing, my stomach is churning and my anxiety levels are rising. It has only been half an hour since I ventured out. School has not even begun. I still have the whole day in front of me. Yet I am already worn down. Exhausted.

At school, I'll have to engage in teen banter with my classmates. While conversation will be effortless for them, I'll struggle to decide which script to use. I'll force myself to make eye contact, to mirror appropriate body language and to vary my facial expressions. I'll try to figure out when to speak, when to smile, when to vary the tone of my voice and what to say next. I'll worry about whether my interaction appears forced, awkward and unnatural. I'll panic about how to conclude the conversation. And all while my vision blurs, my heart races and I begin to feel more and more lightheaded.

The reality is that we live in a world that makes very little effort to understand and accept autistic people. No one should be expected to hide their difficulties to the degree that we're forced to. We shouldn't be expected to silently endure the discomfort and pain caused by our sensory sensitivities and to hide our difficulties with social interaction for fear of being judged and looked down upon. How do we find the right balance between protecting ourselves and being open about our challenges and being free to be ourselves? Unfortunately, there is no easy answer.

I believe that society should be more inclusive, supportive and accepting of people who are different, whether that difference is due to race, ethnicity, gender, sexual orientation, religion or disability. I think it reflects badly on a society when a group of people, such as the autistic community, feel compelled to hide their identity so that they're accepted and treated with dignity and respect. I believe that the best way to make the world more understanding of autistic people and more autism-friendly is by sharing our stories and our experiences. Most neurotypicals don't understand what it's like to be autistic and don't understand how challenging it is to live in a world that isn't designed for you.

It's up to us to educate them.

I've met so many amazing people (autistic and neurotypical) who are passionate about improving the lives of autistic people and who are determined to make things better for us and for future generations of autistic children and young people. I'm sharing my story and my experiences because I believe that one person can make a difference, and I believe that the autistic community has the power to change the way neurotypicals treat us. My hope is that one day autistic people will be understood, accepted and embraced so that we can be free to be ourselves, because we were never meant to fit in; we were meant to stand out.

5

Managing Your Sensory Sensitivities and Sensory Overloads

Having sensory sensitivities is a large part of being autistic. Our sensory issues will never go away. Not being able to filter sensory information can be intolerable, especially at the end of a long day when our defenses have been weakened. Sensory overloads negatively impact us physically and emotionally. Yet since most neurotypicals don't experience sensory overloads, they cannot fully understand how distressing, overwhelming and painful they can be.

I hate supermarkets. I hate the assault of sickly, pungent, acrid, musty and sour smells from fruits and vegetables, mixing with cheese and fish and cleaning products. I hate the screechy wheels of metal shopping carts rattling down the aisle. I hate the bright lights, the claustrophobia-inducing cluttered shelves crammed with multicolored products and the drastic temperature variations between the different aisles.

I hate having to be hypervigilant for excited and energetic young children who may accidentally brush up against me. I hate being in constant fear that there'll be a deafening loudspeaker announcement. I hate the glaring lights, the crinkling of plastic bags, the squelching of footsteps on the glossy floors and the impatient queue at the checkout counter. The list goes on and on and on. It's all too much! The sensory overload can be so overpowering that I desperately want to cover my ears, curl up into a ball and shut out the world.

I have a lot of sympathy for autistic children and young people who are overcome by all the noise and smells and crowds and chaos, especially the autistic child who writhes on the floor in distress because their sensory overload is unbearable. Much too often, neurotypicals assume that we're misbehaving, spoiled and over-indulged. They may even blame our parents for not disciplining us. But what most neurotypical people don't know is that having a reaction to sensory overload is very traumatic and painful, and it is often beyond our control. It can also be extremely embarrassing for the person going through it, especially since many of us are highly aware that some of our reactions are not considered "normal," and that people are judging us. Sometimes, when I'm very distressed and close to a sensory meltdown, I'll talk aloud to myself. I'll tell myself that it'll be okay. I'll recite positive and affirming statements to try to calm and soothe myself. I need to talk aloud because there is too much noise and clutter inside my head. Unfortunately, to neurotypicals who are observing me talking to myself, it may look as if I'm delusional or under the influence of alcohol or drugs. Even though my behavior is mortifying, if talking aloud to myself helps me to survive a sensory overload, then that's what I'm going to do.

Trying to build up sensory tolerance and ignoring sensory sensitivities does not work. However, there are definitely things that can be done to manage your sensory sensitivities so that they have less of a negative effect on your daily life. Below are some suggestions:

- **Create a sensory survival kit.** In my sensory survival kit, I always have a headset. *Always.* I find that listening to music is the key to surviving sensory intolerances. I have several roll-on aromatherapy oils to neutralize nasty smells. I particularly like lavender and ginger. I roll the oil on to my nose to block out unpleasant smells. I have Tiger Balm to rub on my skin in case someone accidentally bumps into me. I find the menthol cools, tingles and soothes the area. I always have two pocket-sized tissue packets, which I place in the two back pockets of my jeans so that I can create a seat cushion when I am sitting in an uncomfortable chair for a long time. I have wet wipes because I hate getting sticky and powdery substances on my hands. I have a menthol lip balm because I dislike the sensation of having dry lips. I also have extra hair bands, which I can discreetly use to fidget with when I get distressed. I have heartburn medication. I also always carry a snack. Your survival kit may look completely different from mine. The important thing is to include items that will help to neutralize some of the unpleasant sensory experiences you regularly encounter. I am always adapting my survival kit for different situations. For example, I change my survival kit to adapt to seasonal changes and for air travel.

- **Listen to music.** My greatest weapon against sensory overloads is music. I find that listening to music distracts me from focusing on my sensory discomfort and helps to block out noise. Listening to music also makes me happy.

- **Communicate.** Make sure that you communicate as much information as you can about your sensory sensitivities. Provide your family, teachers and friends with a detailed description of your particular sensory sensitivities. I often assume that other people experience the world in the same way I do. They don't. It's up to you to spell it out to them. Be very specific. The more information you provide to those around you, the better their understanding will be of your sensory triggers and how they affect you. Once they're aware of your sensory triggers, they'll be in a much better position to support you and help you to manage them.

- **Turn your bedroom into a sensory haven.** Since the outside world can be a traumatic sensory experience, it's important to have a sanctuary. My bedroom is a place where I can go to soothe and calm myself. A place where I can recharge. There are no fluorescent lights and unpleasant noises and smells. It's a place I can completely control. When creating your sensory haven, design it so the space works for you. Small changes can have major results. Keep in mind that different colors can create different moods. I've painted my room a grayish blue because shades of blue are supposed to be more relaxing. Determine whether you feel more positive, relaxed and in control when your room is messy or tidy. I feel better when my room is tidy and so I try to keep it that way. The most important thing is to create a room that has positive energy, where you feel comfortable and secure. I don't like to bring negative energy into my positive space. So if I'm having a bad time at school, I don't do my homework in my bedroom. There are many ways to bring positive vibes and associations into your room. For example, if I buy a Kylie Lip Kit or something else I have been eagerly awaiting, I open the package in my room. I play music in my bedroom all the time. I also always have my trusted companion Rico in my room.

- **Get plenty of sleep.** Like many autistic people, I have trouble sleeping. Sometimes it's because I'm obsessively worrying about something. If you're being kept awake by a worry, write it down on a piece of paper, fold it several times and place it on the floor by your bedroom door. Tell yourself that there's nothing more you can do about it and that you'll try to sort it out in the morning.

  Some people find that melatonin sprays or tablets help them to fall asleep. I swear by weighted blankets. Initially, I was skeptical, but I've been converted. I have a soft, fluffy, gray ten-pound weighted blanket that provides just enough pressure to anchor, calm and soothe me. If you frequently have trouble sleeping, I highly recommend that you try one. It's also important to get into the right state of mind. If you're a visual thinker, visualize your perfect place. Focus on what you see, what you can smell and hear and how you feel. If any bad thoughts creep in, banish them and focus on your perfect place. This will help to calm and soothe you and make it easier for you to fall asleep.

- **Use your clothes as a shield.** My skin is particularly sensitive, especially to wind and temperature variations. I try to cover my skin as much as possible because I hate the sensation of someone lightly brushing against my skin. It feels like hundreds of insects are crawling on the area where I was touched. I find that clothing is a great way to create a protective barrier. I rarely wear shorts or tank tops, even on a blisteringly hot summer day. I always layer and try to wear a front-zip hoodie, so that I have an additional layer of clothing if I get cold, *and* I have a makeshift cushion if I have to sit on an uncomfortable chair.

- **Manage your anxiety.** The best way to prevent your sensory sensitivities from getting out of control is by managing your anxiety. I find that when my anxiety levels are high, my sensory sensitivities become much worse. Suddenly, I'm unable to tolerate things that usually don't bother me. My sensory intolerances have been at their absolute worse when I've been bullied. Sometimes situations that cause us anxiety are out of our control, but, where possible, reducing your anxiety will also reduce your sensory overloads.

- **Avoid places that trigger sensory overloads.**
  There are some places that are a sensory
  nightmare. For me, it's supermarkets. I also hate
  gas stations. I loathe the smell of gasoline. It's
  usually easy to avoid going to places that trigger
  your sensory overloads. Having said that, it's
  important that you don't make your list too long,
  because otherwise there's a danger you'll never
  venture beyond your doorstep.

I hope that some of these suggestions will be helpful.
Don't be afraid to modify them and to experiment with
different options until you identify techniques and
solutions that work for you.

SENSITIVITY TO LIGHT

I'm very sensitive to light. If you're sensitive too, I
highly recommend that you invest in a pair of good-
quality polarized sunglasses. Be sure to experiment with
different tinted lenses so that you can find a color tint
that works for you. If you wear prescription glasses, I
recommend that you get prescription sunglasses. I wear
my sunglasses outdoors all the time. Not only do they
look cool, but they also really help to protect against
visual overloads.

The most common source of light sensitivity is
fluorescent lights. Fluorescent lighting is really intense
and harsh. I hate fluorescent lights. They flicker and
emit a low-pitched hum that most people can't hear.
I find the flickering and hum extremely distracting.
They can also cause me to feel nauseous, get headaches

and feel dizzy. Unfortunately, avoiding fluorescent lighting is almost impossible because most places have fluorescent lighting, especially schools. However, I have found that Irlen glasses have really helped. The colored lenses filter out wavelengths of light that create visual stress and overload.

SENSITIVITY TO SOUND

I have very sensitive hearing. Loud sounds can cause me physical pain. But even soft sounds can be distressing. I hate the sound of footsteps, the humming of electricity, whistling, any kind of slamming, the sound of something that has been dropped, running water, extractor fans, the sound a zipper makes, the tapping of feet, slurping (even saying the word is unpleasant), the sound of the words "queue" and "conundrum," the cracking of knuckles, the sound of plumbing, clocks ticking, the sound of my heartbeat, the sound of metal clashing... The list is infinite!

I also have difficulty filtering out background noise. When I'm in a crowded place, such as a restaurant or at school, I can get overwhelmed by people's conversations. Voices are magnified. I can hear each of their conversations, which can lead to feeling as if I'm about to short-circuit. For example, on the subway I can hear dozens of people's conversations. I can hear their breathing and the chewing of gum. I can hear the music leaking from their headsets, their footsteps and the rustling of newspapers. I find it impossible to screen out the extraneous noise, especially when I get anxious. Ironically, the more anxious I get, the more sensitive my hearing becomes, which then makes me even more anxious. It's a vicious circle. It's for this reason that I use music to block the noise. As I said earlier, listening to music is my greatest weapon against auditory overloads.

The only way to prevent auditory overloads is to avoid going to loud and crowded places. If you want to go somewhere that might be loud and crowded, I suggest that you plan ahead and get creative. For example, if you're going to a restaurant, go at a time when it's less likely to be busy or ask to sit in a quieter section. If you want to go to a theme park, go on a day when it's raining—there are likely to be fewer people.

When I'm at school and I get overwhelmed by boisterous teens, I like to escape to the library or the medical center—quiet and calm places where I can compose myself and recharge. Another way of filtering out distressing sounds is to wear noise-cancelling headsets. They're very good at neutralizing and filtering out noise.

SENSITIVITY TO SMELL

I have a very sensitive sense of smell. It is likely you do too. I have a strong aversion to certain odors that I find repulsive—for example, the smell of gasoline, Sharpie pens, glue, Coca-Cola, Sauerkraut, tuna, people's breath, artificial strawberry scents, most cleaning products, most perfumes and the smell of taxis (the smell of lots of people in a confined space). On the flip side, my acute sense of smell also means that I can really enjoy and appreciate smells too. I love the smell of books, of freshly cut grass, wet paint and burning wood. The best way to neutralize offensive smells is to have aromatherapy sprays and roll-ons in your survival kit. Rolling the oil on to your nose will help to block out unpleasant smells.

SENSITIVITY TO TEXTURES AND TASTE

Autistic children are notorious for being picky eaters. Many autistic children have a restrictive diet because they find most foods intolerable. This is partly due to the texture of certain foods. I really dislike slimy foods, such as cooked tomatoes, cucumbers, canned fruit and okra. I also really dislike the texture of foam and anything sprinkled with powdered sugar. As long as you're eating a balanced diet, don't feel bad about eating a limited range of foods. You're not being unadventurous or difficult; you're accommodating your sensory sensitivities. Another important point to consider in relation to food is that it is extremely common for autistic people to have stomach and intestinal problems. It may be that you're avoiding certain foods because your body doesn't tolerate them very well. I've found that avoiding dairy products has helped reduce my stomach problems.

SENSITIVITY TO TOUCH

Autistic children are also notorious for their tactile sensitivities, which can range from being under-sensitive to being over-sensitive. My sister happens to be under-sensitive. She has a high threshold for pain and barely feels the cold. She goes out in the dead of winter wearing a flimsy summer dress and often refuses to wear a coat (which really bothers my mom). When she was younger, she would hug us really tightly and would insist that my mom squeeze her hand harder and harder, because she claimed that she couldn't feel her hand being held. My sister loved to wear clothes that were way too tight and small for her. She was also frequently hungry, even immediately after she had just eaten. She claimed she didn't feel full. As my sister has gotten older, her under-sensitivity has improved.

I'm the polar opposite of my sister. I'm over-sensitive. I find touch so uncomfortable and painful that I dislike being touched and avoid touching others. Even greeting someone with a handshake is painful and distressing. I've only recently learned to tolerate being hugged. There was a time when I couldn't wear my hair down. The sensation of having my hair brush against my neck or face felt like being sliced with shards of glass. I am still traumatized by an incident that happened in nursery school. We were using glue for an art project.

I accidentally spilled white PVA glue all over my hands. I was desperate to get it off my hands and asked my teacher for permission to wash my hands. She refused. She told me that there was no point because I would only end up getting more glue on my hands. I was distraught. I remember spending the rest of the activity crying (something I rarely do). I was despondent about having the horrendous sensation of sticky, gooey glue hardening on my skin.

If you're over-sensitive, you may have trouble tolerating clothes tags and seams, wool, synthetic materials (such as nylon and polyester), lace and elastics. This can make buying clothes that don't cause discomfort or pain very challenging. We're often very restricted in what we can wear, especially since many of us find man-made synthetic materials itchy and scratchy. I've learned to buy clothes made from natural, breathable fabrics, such as fabrics made of 100% organic cotton. One trick that has really helped me is to wash clothes many, many times with an unscented non-bio laundry detergent before wearing them. I find that this makes them so much softer and more comfortable to wear.

SENSITIVITY TO SIGHTS

Many autistic people are visual thinkers. We can recall a vivid image of what we have seen. It's as if our mind takes a photograph. A great benefit to being a visual thinker is that you can use this ability to alter your mood and lift your spirits. If you want to feel better, look at an image that makes you feel happy. Look at a photo of your family on an awesome holiday or pictures of puppies or pandas or of nature. When you're feeling down, an easy way to boost your mood is to recall these images and focus on them. I like to recall unflattering images of my dog Rico fast asleep, with his tongue sticking out. This image of him always makes me smile. Next time you're feeling down, try recalling an image that will make you smile.

While there are many benefits to being a visual thinker, there is also a major drawback. If we see something unpleasant, the negative image will be etched in our memory and can haunt us. I sometimes inadvertently end up watching a few seconds of a horror-movie trailer when watching something unrelated on YouTube. For example, I saw the diabolical clown from Stephen King's *It* movie when the trailer unexpectedly appeared on my screen. The image petrifies me! Especially since it pops into my head at the most unexpected times. Unfortunately, there is no way of erasing the image. If you're a visual thinker too, be careful about what you look at. I would suggest that you avoid watching horror movies or gory crime dramas.

AUTISM-FRIENDLY SAFE SPACES

Some businesses and public places are finally starting to recognize that autistic people's lives can sometimes be severely curtailed by their sensory sensitivities and have started to create a more welcoming and inclusive environment for us. In England, some supermarket chains and shopping malls have introduced a "quiet hour" for autistic shoppers who struggle with noise and crowds. The supermarkets dim the lights, turn off the music, reduce the use of trolleys, turn off the loudspeaker and turn down the checkout beeps. Many nationwide cinemas have also introduced regular autism-friendly screenings. Museums and airports are also starting to accommodate autistic people. Some airports, including Heathrow Airport and Ireland's Shannon Airport, have created sensory rooms or quiet rooms for autistic children. Although we are still a long way from living in a society that creates a supportive and inclusive environment for autistic people, autism quiet hours and safe spaces are a step in the right direction.

6

Taking Care of Your Body

One of the common stereotypes that neurotypicals have about autistic girls is that we're all uninterested in how we look and that we're all disheveled and poorly groomed. This isn't true. Just as with neurotypical girls, there's a huge range among autistic girls. Some of us are very conscious of our appearance and some of us are uninterested in how we look. However, most of us fall somewhere in between.

Appearances are important because most people base their impressions on how you look. The most important aspect of your appearance is maintaining good hygiene. Good personal hygiene and grooming is an expected social norm. Future dates and future employers will expect you to be clean and well groomed. So why not get into good habits now?

Personal hygiene and grooming can present issues for autistic girls. Our sensory sensitivities can make grooming unpleasant, especially if you dislike the sensation of water on your skin or the sensation of brushing your hair and teeth. Some of us also have motor coordination problems that make some things more difficult, such as washing and brushing our hair. However, it's important to keep clean. Unfortunately, if you look unkept and smell bad, it is very likely you will be teased and bullied. Good hygiene is also important for your general health and your confidence.

When you start to go through puberty, you'll find that your body will begin to smell in ways it didn't before, especially your armpits. The best way to avoid smelling bad is to take a daily shower or bath. If you're sensitive to heavily scented soaps and body washes, try using an unscented soap or body wash. Dove has a good selection. Make sure you pay particular attention to your underarms and your pubic area (the V-shaped area between your hip bones and your legs). Since soap can irritate the pubic area, instead of using soap you may want to just use a wet washcloth to gently clean the area.

I recommend that you perfect the two-minute shower. If I've had a particularly stressful day and I'm experiencing sensory overload, the sensation of water coming through a high-pressure shower head can feel as if I'm standing under Niagara Falls. It can be very painful! On those days, I either take a record-speed shower or I take a bath. If I am having a very, very bad sensory day and there is no conceivable way that I can tolerate the sound of water, temperature variations and water pressure on my skin, I clean myself with wet wipes or body wipes. Body wipes remove sweat, dirt and body odor—often they're used for camping and festivals where there aren't washing facilities. They are sold in some shops or are available online, including on Amazon.

If you have difficulties with time management, it can sometimes be tricky to know how long you have been in the shower. One hack I use to ensure that I don't lose track of time when taking a shower is to ceate playlists that I use to measure increments of time. For example, I have a ten-minute playlist and a 15-minute playlist. Listening to music also has the added effect that it helps to block out the noise of splashing water, a noise I dislike. If you think you could benefit from this hack, I suggest that you invest in an inexpensive waterproof speaker or waterproof radio that you can use in the shower.

Unless your hair is greasy, it isn't necessary to wash it every day. You can wash your hair every two or three days. If you're concerned about getting shampoo in your eyes, buy a gentle shampoo that is formulated so that it doesn't sting if it gets in your eyes—for example, Johnson's No More Tears Baby Shampoo. I particularly like their natural lavender shampoo. Sometimes you may find that you use too much shampoo or too little. If you're having a difficult time determining how much to use, I suggest you buy a plastic bottle with a pump and transfer your shampoo into it. Once you determine how many pumps is an ideal amount of shampoo for you to wash your hair, you can automatically pump that amount every time you wash your hair. It's a great way to take the guesswork out of how much shampoo you need to use.

If the towels you have at home are rough and scratchy, I highly recommend replacing them with a softer alternative. Some towels can feel as if you're drying yourself with sandpaper. I've found that towels made from bamboo are incredibly soft and absorbent.

Another important way to maintain good hygiene and avoid smelling bad is to apply a deodorant or antiperspirant after you take a shower. Deodorants come in lots of different forms. If you hate having sticky, gooey substances on your skin, you may want to avoid using gel or roll-on deodorants. If you hate the sensation of dry, powdery substances on your skin, you may want to avoid aerosol spray deodorants. I avoid them because I dislike having powdery, cakey substances on my skin and I dislike inhaling the airborne powder. I prefer to use liquid deodorants that have a pump spray. My favorite is Burt's Bees 100% All-Natural Deodorant with Sage Oil.

STARTING A SKINCARE ROUTINE

During puberty, your body produces more oil, which can clog your pores and cause pimples. The best way to prevent breakouts is to wash your face every morning and every night with a gentle facial cleanser that will help to remove any excess oil. I avoid using anything with microbeads, both for environmental reasons (the tiny beads end up contaminating the ocean and are ingested by sea life) and because I don't like the sensation of scouring my skin with abrasive grains.

There are so many products to choose from that it can be a bit overwhelming. I have found that I tolerate natural, unscented, organic products the best. I use a cleanser by Lush called 9 to 5. It's mild and has a neutral scent. I avoid using any products that contain alcohol. Products containing alcohol are harsh, can over-dry your skin and have a nasty smell.

If you have a mild breakout, try using an acne product. Most acne products contain benzoyl peroxide, which can be effective, but they can also irritate sensitive skin. Alternatively, try using a more natural alternative, such as a product containing witch hazel. I'm a fan of Thayers Alcohol-Free Rose Petal Witch Hazel with Aloe Vera.

BRUSHING YOUR TEETH

Brushing your teeth can be a sensory nightmare. However, there are ways to make the experience less unpleasant. It may be that you prefer the sensation of using an electric toothbrush. I don't like the vibration sensation and so prefer a manual toothbrush. When choosing a toothbrush, it's important to select one that has the right bristle strength for your sensitivities. I prefer soft and rounded bristles. If you currently dislike brushing your teeth, I suggest that you experiment by trying out a range of different toothbrushes, including toothbrushes with different shaped bristles and different bristle strengths. You may also want to try an alternative to nylon bristles. The Curaprox CS5460 Ultra Soft Toothbrush has ultra-fine, polyester filament bristles that are much gentler on gums and teeth than regular nylon bristles. It may take some trial and error, but once you find the right toothbrush, you'll be less reluctant to brush your teeth.

Another aspect of oral hygiene that may cause some discomfort is toothpaste. Toothpastes can have a very strong and overpowering taste. Most toothpastes have a strong flavor of spearmint or peppermint. They can also be gritty and leave you with a burning sensation. There are lots of gentler alternatives that are less likely to aggravate your sensory issues. I prefer to use charcoal toothpaste or fruit-flavored toothpaste. I find that they have a milder taste. For example, Colgate's Natural Extracts collection comes in charcoal and fresh lemon.

VISITING THE DENTIST

Visiting the dentist can be a distressing experience for anyone, but the bright lights, the strong smells and the ear-splitting sounds of the dental drill are especially distressing if you're autistic. Also, our mouths are extremely sensitive. The feeling of a latex-gloved hand in your mouth and the sensation of a cold metal dental drill or instrument can be very uncomfortable, if not painful. One way to reduce your distress is to wear dark sunglasses and to wear a headset so that you can block out the sounds of the dental equipment by listening to soothing music. If you dislike the feeling of being moved backwards, ask the dentist or hygienist to lean the chair back before you get on it. If you benefit from weighted blankets, you may want to ask if you can wear their X-ray vest—its weight might make you feel more anchored and help to calm you. My biggest tip is to ask the dentist to explain everything that she/he is going to do, so that you have a concrete idea of what to expect. I find this helps me to feel more in control.

THE ART OF SHAVING

As you go through puberty, you may notice that the hair on your underarms and legs starts to become coarser and darker. In some cultures, teen girls are expected to shave their underarms and legs. I began to shave my underarms and legs to stop girls from teasing me about my dark leg hair. If you decide to shave, here are some tips to avoid nicks and razor burn:

- Shave in a warm shower or bathtub. Water hydrates and softens the skin, making it easier to shave without getting a nick.

- Apply a generous amount of a lubricant, such as shaving cream, shower gel or bar soap. If you hate the texture and feel of shaving cream or shower gel, try using baby oil instead. Be very careful, though: oil can make the shower and bathroom floor very slippery. Whatever you do, don't shave dry! It can seriously irritate your skin.

- Shave in the direction of hair growth, such as in a downward direction on the leg since leg hair grows down. This will help to prevent razor burn.

- Don't rush. It's important to shave slowly and gently. Let the razor blade do the work. Don't rush or push down too hard with the razor— you're likely to cut yourself.

- Don't forget to shave the parts of your legs that you can't see, like the back of your legs.

- Change your razors frequently. A dull blade can irritate your skin and cause rashes. I strongly recommend that you avoid using cheap, disposable razors and that you invest in a quality razor with conditioning strips and a pivoting head.

- Be especially cautious around the knee and ankle area. Their odd shape makes it very easy to cut these areas.

There are other hair removal options that I find less appealing, such as waxing and depilatories. Since waxing involves getting slathered with hot and sticky melted wax and then ripping the wax off, it's a sensory nightmare. Waxing is also painful. A depilatory is a cream that dissolves hair. You smear the cream on to your skin and leave it for a few minutes. When you rinse it off, the hair washes off too. The problem with depilatories is that they can cause skin irritation and they stink.

THAT TIME OF THE MONTH
Period Basics

Periods can be distressing for autistic girls, because they are messy, unpredictable and can be painful. The word "period" is short for menstrual period—the period of time when blood flows out of a girl's or woman's vagina. The amount of blood varies from four to six tablespoons. Periods usually last about five days. But a period can be shorter or last longer. When you first get your period, it may not come regularly. At first, the length of time between each period and the number of days the blood flow lasts may change from one month to the next. Eventually, your periods will become more regular.

Period Products

There are three types of period products that you can use. You may need to experiment a bit to find which product works best for you.

- **Pads.** Most girls use a pad when they first get their period, because they are convenient and easy to use. Pads come in lots of different shapes and sizes. The pads have a sticky strip that attaches to your underwear. Some have "wings" that wrap around the edges of your underwear for added protection. The pads are made of an absorbent material that soaks up the blood as it leaves your body. Since autistic girls have sensory sensitivities, you may find wearing a pad uncomfortable. It is worth experimenting with different brands, sizes, thicknesses and shapes. One way of avoiding sensory discomfort is to change your pads regularly. Always remember to dispose of your pads properly. Used pads should be wrapped up and put into the wastebasket. Do not try flushing them in the toilet; pads will block the toilet.

  Another option you may want to consider are washable, reusable pads or sanitary towels, especially since they are generally made of natural fibers such as cotton and bamboo. If you have a sensory intolerance to synthetic materials and chemicals, reusable pads may be a better option for you. Another benefit of reusable pads is that they are more environmentally friendly and are also less expensive in the long run. They can be bought online, including on Amazon.

- **Tampons.** Some girls prefer to use tampons, a cotton plug that a girl inserts into her vagina to absorb the blood before it leaves her body. Most tampons come with an applicator that guides the tampon into place. A string hangs outside of your body so that you can pull the tampon out. Tampons come in different sizes and absorbencies. Since tampons are inserted into your vagina, you can pee without having to remove it (pee comes out of your urethra, a different opening). One of the benefits of using a tampon is that you can swim during your period. It's very important to change your tampon regularly and to never leave it in for more than eight hours because this can increase your risk of a serious infection called toxic shock syndrome.

- **Menstrual cup.** Some girls prefer to use a menstrual cup that you can insert into your vagina. The cup holds the blood until you empty it.

Most pads and tampons are available in deodorant and non-deodorant versions. The deodorant versions have perfumes and other chemicals to fight odor. However, they can cause irritation and allergic reactions, and can exacerbate sensory sensitivities. I recommend that you use unscented products and change your pads regularly to manage any concerns you may have about odor. I also recommend that you buy a cute little bag where you can store your period products and keep it somewhere handy, such as in your backpack or your locker.

Many autistic girls have an aversion to using public toilets or the toilets at school. This can be especially challenging when you're on your period. If you don't use public toilets or the toilets at school, I recommend that you wear a super-absorbent night-time pad. I also recommend that you wear period-proof underwear. Thinx (USA) and Modibodi (UK) make washable, reusable underwear that can replace pads and tampons. They come in different absorbencies and different styles (bikini, thong, boy short and brief). If you're sensitive to fabrics and materials, Thinx period-proof underwear is available in organic cotton (go to www.shethinx.com). I also recommend that you wear black or dark-colored clothing. Whatever you do, avoid wearing white.

Period Apps

Most autistic individuals aren't very good at keeping track of time. We also like our structure and routines. Since periods can be unpredictable, autistic girls can find this upsetting. The best way to predict when your period is due is to track your periods using an app on your phone. I highly recommend Clue, a period app that tracks your periods and sends you a notification so that you're less likely to be taken by surprise. There are also many other similar apps that you can experiment with.

Managing Premenstrual Syndrome (PMS)

PMS is a group of physical and emotional symptoms associated with your menstrual cycle. You may find that you experience headaches, joint and muscle aches, backaches, breast tenderness, insomnia, constipation or diarrhea and stomach cramps. To make matters worse, many of us find that our sensory sensitivities skyrocket, which can significantly exacerbate our symptoms. Our emotions are also affected. You may find that you have difficulty controlling your emotions and that your emotions and anxiety are magnified. You may experience mood swings and irritability. You may also feel cranky, tired and upset, and have trouble concentrating. In other words, PMS can be very unpleasant.

There are a few things you can do to make your PMS symptoms less unpleasant. For starters, make sure you get plenty of sleep and rest. For stomach cramps, I highly recommend a lavender-scented microwavable wheat bag, which you can place on your stomach to soothe your cramps. You may find that having a warm cup of caffeine-free chamomile tea can also ease your symptoms. You may also want to take painkillers or anti-inflammatory medication to help reduce discomfort caused by headaches or joint and muscle pain, such as ibuprofen or paracetamol. You may want to consider medication that has been specifically formulated for PMS, such as Feminax (UK) and Pamprin and Midol (USA). I find that it also really helps to understand why you are having these symptoms and how long they will last. Knowing how PMS affects you helps you to feel more in control of your body.

Period Etiquette

There is a social etiquette in relation to talking about periods. Although it's fine to talk about periods, there's a time and a place. It's better to be private and discreet. Don't announce to mixed company that you are wearing a pad or are on your period. Publicly talking about periods can make most people uncomfortable, especially boys. However, you can discuss your period with your mom, girlfriends and the school nurse. It's also appropriate to share that you are on your period if it's relevant information, such as if you're required to swim at school. In this situation, it's appropriate to discreetly tell the gym teacher that you're on your period so that you can be excused from swimming.

7

Understanding Your Emotions and Looking After Your Mental Health

Do you find it challenging to identify and talk about the emotions that you're feeling? You're not alone. If you're anything like me, you may struggle with identifying and expressing your emotions. It's very common in autistic people. Many autistics have difficulty identifying, describing and processing their emotions. This difficulty is called **alexithymia** (which literally means having no words for emotions).

Alexithymia is characterized by three main difficulties:

- difficulties in identifying what you're feeling
- difficulties in describing your feelings to others
- difficulties in distinguishing between your feelings and the physical sensations related to an emotional response (for example, a rapid

heartbeat, trouble breathing or the sensation of having the fluttery feeling of butterflies in your stomach).

As someone who is alexithymic, I know how stressful it can be when a person asks you how you're feeling and you don't know how to respond. My response is always "I'm fine." Since most neurotypicals are in tune with their emotions, I avoid telling people that I frequently don't know how I'm feeling or don't know how to describe how I'm feeling. I suspect that most people would find this baffling. I can generally distinguish between big emotions, such as feeling good or bad and feeling happy or sad, but anything in between is murky and muddled. I find it particularly difficult to identify and describe the more subtle and intricate emotions—for example, distinguishing between envy and jealousy.

This may sound strange, but one thing I've noticed is that I can identify my feelings through music. I've found that I unconsciously choose to listen to a specific song when I'm feeling a particular emotion. Eventually, a pattern emerges that gives me enough information to be able to identify the emotion that is linked to that particular song. For example, whenever I get blood drawn (something that I absolutely hate having done), I listen to the song "Love" by Lana Del Rey. I now know that whenever I have the urge to listen to the song "Love" I'm feeling apprehensive and scared.

Expressing my emotions is something I also struggle with. Although expressing emotions comes naturally to neurotypicals, to me it feels foreign and unnatural. Even when I'm able to express my emotions, I often find that my facial expressions and body language don't match up with how I'm feeling. Sometimes there's a huge disconnect. I could be feeling ecstatic inside, yet my face could have an expression of indifference or, worse yet, boredom. It's as if my emotions and my body are completely detached from each other.

Since my emotions rarely match my facial expressions and body language, this often leads to misunderstandings. People constantly ask me whether I am sad or upset or bored. I find it frustrating, because the facial expression others attribute to me rarely reflects my mood. I am constantly being misunderstood. When my younger sister Kiera was four (and I was eight), she was speeding down the sidewalk on her micro scooter, caught the edge of an uneven slab of stone and catapulted headfirst on to the hard ground. By the time my mom and I caught up with her, she had a huge lump on her forehead. We watched as the lump continued to balloon in front of our eyes. It looked as if her forehead was being inflated. Kiera was screaming and my mom was in a state of panic, and yet I was calm and collected. Perhaps even a little aloof. I would later be accused of not showing appropriate concern and of being a bit callous and uncaring. It wasn't that I didn't care about my sister or that I didn't realize the seriousness of the situation; I just respond very differently from other people.

In addition to my feelings and my facial expressions rarely matching, I also have a time delay when it comes to identifying and processing my emotions. Sometimes it's not until hours or even days later that I am able to process and make sense of my emotions. This is especially true of intense emotional experiences, such as when I have been bullied. There have been lots of occasions when I was unable to express and communicate how I felt at the precise moment when the bullying incident was being investigated. While my bullies faked tears, distress and remorse in an over-the-top performance worthy of an Oscar (a coveted acting award), I appeared cold, detached and unemotional. Inevitably, the school staff would be forgiving and lenient with the bullies and would be mistrustful of me. Since I did not react in the conventional way they were expecting, I made them uneasy and suspicious of me. I have even been accused of lying or embellishing my story, simply because I didn't appear to be appropriately distraught. Yet if the staff had been able to tap into how I was feeling, they would have discovered that I was distressed and traumatized, despite my stoic and composed exterior.

If you're alexithymic and someone accuses you of not showing an appropriate emotional response, I suggest that you explain to them that not all people show their emotions in the same way. Reassure them that even though it may have appeared that you were not concerned, this is absolutely not the case. Explain that it also takes you longer to respond to emotional situations. If you struggle to communicate your emotions in a face-to-face conversation, you may want to try expressing yourself in writing. I find that I'm more eloquent and expressive if I'm given time to reflect on my feelings and have the option of expressing my emotions on paper or by email.

SOCIAL ANXIETY

Most autistic girls suffer from social anxiety. Social anxiety might as well be my shadow. It's my constant companion. It's not that we're born with social anxiety; we develop it as a form of self-protection. I think our social anxiety stems from our difficulty in understanding social situations and from years of social blunders and missteps that often result in us being misunderstood, judged, mistreated, ridiculed and bullied. Eventually, our negative social experiences and our fear of not knowing what to say or what to do in social situations make us weary. Social anxiety serves an important purpose for autistic girls: it reminds us to stay on our toes.

Another aspect that most people don't understand about autistic girls, and which neurotypicals rarely take into consideration, is that we have a limited amount of energy that we can devote to social communication. I like to refer to this as our social battery. Our social anxiety is tied to our social battery. When our social battery is fully charged, we're at our social best. As the social battery starts to drain, our social skills deteriorate until we reach the limit of our ability to socially interact. Social interaction comes at a price. It leaves us physically and emotionally spent. The only way for us to recover is to have time to ourselves so that we can recuperate and recharge.

When I'm at school, I try to ration my social battery so that it lasts the entire day. I'm constantly struggling to find the right balance between socializing and safeguarding my social battery so that it doesn't empty before I get home. There are times when my rationing fails. If I have to cope with an unexpected change in my schedule or routine, have to partake in group conversations involving teen banter or have to attend a mandatory after-school club, my ability to socialize will reach critical levels and my anxiety levels will skyrocket.

When my social battery drains and my anxiety reaches critical levels, my ability to function drastically deteriorates. I become a lot clumsier, less tolerant of being touched, more rigid in my thinking, less able to cope with any changes in my schedule or routine and more sensitive to lights, noise and smells. Things that don't normally interfere with my ability to function become a huge challenge.

It is unlikely that you will be able to banish social anxiety from your life. Unfortunately, it is something you're going to have to learn to live with. However, there are strategies you can use to prevent your anxiety from reaching critical levels. Here are some of the strategies that I use to manage my anxiety:

- **Alone time.** One of the best ways for us to recharge and relax is through solitude. We need time to ourselves, away from sensory experiences and away from the pressures of social interaction. After a long day at school, I need at least an hour in my room to recover and recharge from what is often a very demanding day. If you need alone time at school to reduce your anxiety, ask a teacher if she can provide a place for you to go, a safe and secluded area at school that you can use as a sanctuary during break times and during lunch time, such as the school library or any empty classroom.

- **Pets.** Spending time with my dog immediately lowers my anxiety. When I'm with Rico, I don't have to worry about being judged for saying or doing the wrong thing. I don't have to pretend to fit into other people's definition of "normal." Rico loves me unconditionally, and I love him unconditionally back. Our relationship is simple and straightforward. When I am anxious, I stroke Rico's soft, fluffy coat, and I immediately feel calmer and more serene. At night, when I am wide awake and he is snuggled next to me, his breathing can sometimes lull me to sleep. Even if I'm struggling to fall asleep, his presence soothes me. If you don't already have a pet, I highly recommend that you get one.

- **Music.** If I could, I would listen to music *all* the time. Music is my biggest weapon against anxiety. I listen to music to distract myself from focusing on my anxiety and from obsessing about my sensory discomfort and intrusive thoughts. Focusing on the lyrics of a song and visualizing the music video allows me to escape. I often rely on music to shut out external noise that could otherwise lead to a sensory overload.

- **Intense interests.** Immersing yourself in your intense interest is a great way to distract yourself and to escape from your everyday worries. Our interests get a bad rap. When neurotypical people have an intense interest, it's referred to as a "passion" and it's encouraged. Yet when autistic people have an intense interest, it's referred to as a "special" interest and it's looked down on and discouraged. Greta Thunberg, the Swedish autistic climate change activist, is proving that autistic "special" interests shouldn't be viewed as a negative characteristic. She's a perfect example of how an autistic person's intense interests can have merit, value and the potential to make a significant contribution to society. In Greta's case, her intense interest in climate change has been the catalyst that inspired over a million young people in over 100 countries around the world to join her in a demonstration on 24 May 2019 to demand that governments reduce their carbon emissions in accordance with the Paris Agreement.

My intense interests are a source of great enjoyment for me. I find that when I lose myself in my intense interest, I can shut out the world. Absorbing yourself in your intense interest also has the benefit of being highly enjoyable and satisfying. One of my intense interests is reading psychology studies. I know it may sound like an odd thing to be interested in, but I genuinely find it fascinating and incredibly rewarding to learn about human behavior. Whatever your intense interest may be, I highly recommend that you use it as a form of escape.

- **Stimming.** Stims are a wide variety of self-stimulating behaviors that autistic people use when they are very anxious or are distressed by a sensory overload. Stimming can be a repetitive motion (such as hand flapping or rocking), repetition of words or phrases or even the repetitive movement of objects. Since most neurotypicals don't understand why we stim, they try to discourage us from doing so. From their perspective, we're acting strangely and need to learn to act "normally." Although stimming may seem alarming or odd to neurotypicals, these behaviors serve an important purpose. Most of us stim because it calms us and helps to alleviate our high levels of anxiety. It's our form of meditation. I find that jiggling my knee is an effective way of reducing my anxiety and of counteracting an overwhelming sensory environment, without bringing too much attention to myself. I also fidget with a hairband that I always wear as a bracelet.

• **Exercise.** Exercising is a great way to reduce anxiety. The benefit of exercise is something I only recently discovered. I used to hate physical activity. I have always been very uncoordinated and clumsy, which caused me a lot of unpleasantness. If I wasn't being teased and ridiculed by my classmates, my PE teachers were accusing me of not trying hard enough or apparently finding endless ways to humiliate me. I was the kid who was always last to be picked for the team and always the first to be out. The kid no one wanted on their team. Needless to say, I didn't have the best relationship with exercise. However, a few months ago I started going to the gym. Initially, it was a chore, but I gradually grew to love it. I especially enjoy exercising on the cycling and elliptical machines. I like that I can go at my own pace and that I can exercise while listening to music. I have found that exercise is a great way of releasing stress, clearing your thoughts and increasing your energy levels. It can also help improve the quality of your sleep.

- **Diet.** Although I love junk food and I could live on chocolate, it is important to have a healthy and balanced diet. A diet that includes vegetables, fruits, complex carbohydrates, lean meats and nuts has a positive effect on our physical health, quality of sleep and anxiety levels. A balanced diet can sometimes pose challenges for autistic individuals who are sensitive to the texture, smell, temperature, color and taste of certain foods. If you have a limited range of foods you can tolerate, you may want to try tricking your body into allowing you to broaden the range of foods you can eat. For example, try modifying your food by pureeing it.

- **Sleep.** Sleep plays an important role in our physical and mental health. Unfortunately, many of us have trouble sleeping. We often take a long time to fall asleep, especially if we're obsessing about events that took place that day or are worrying about tomorrow. The depth and quality of our sleep can also be affected, which means that we're often tired and sleep-deprived. If you're having trouble sleeping, I recommend that you try sleeping with a weighted blanket. I have found that using a combination of melatonin, lavender spray (Lush's Twilight is a firm favorite) and a weighted blanket really helps.

- **Positive attitude.** It's important to try to stay upbeat and to focus on the good aspects of your life. Positive thinking helps to clear your mind of negative self-talk. Even if you've had a particularly tough day, you can always find something to be grateful for. For me, it's my family and my dog. Before I go to sleep, I always try to think of three positive things that happened that day. I also find it empowering to remind myself that even if I'm having a difficult time, it's only temporary and things will improve.

ANXIETY

Anxiety is the feeling you have when you're worried or afraid about things that are about to happen or that could happen. It's a natural human response, which we experience through our thoughts, feelings and physical sensations. There may be times when your social anxiety turns into something bigger, a more generalized and all-encompassing form of anxiety that extends further than your worries about social interaction. Although it's natural to feel anxious some of the time, anxiety can become a mental health issue if it prevents you from being able to live your life as fully as you want to. For example, if:

- your fears or worries are out of proportion to the situation

- you avoid situations that might cause you to feel anxious

- your worries feel very distressing or are hard to control

- you regularly experience anxiety symptoms, such as panic attacks, difficulty breathing, rapid heartbeat and stomach aches

- you find it hard to go about your everyday life or do things you enjoy.

I'm generally able to keep my anxiety levels within a manageable range. However, there have been a few occasions when my anxiety has temporarily taken over my life. For example, after months of being badly bullied, I developed severe anxiety. I began to suffer from daily panic attacks that left me struggling to catch my breath. I also began to suffer from heart palpitations and excruciating stomach aches and headaches, and I was unable to eat and sleep. It was a physical and emotional tornado that left me feeling that my life was spiraling out of control. My parents eventually decided to move me to a different school. As soon as I left the school where I was being bullied, all the extreme symptoms that had been plaguing me disappeared.

If you find that the strategies to manage your anxiety that I suggested are not working and that your anxiety is getting the better of you, you may want to explore the possibility of taking anti-anxiety medication. Before taking any prescription medication, I strongly suggest that you first address any problems you may be having at school or at home that could be triggering your anxiety. For example, if your anxiety is being caused by bullying or by not being adequately supported at school, you should first try addressing these issues.

 Autistic people are often prone to anxiety and other mental health problems.

 This can be due to things like sensory overload, or navigating a world that can be scary and chaotic.

 Because of our difficulties in social situations, it can be easy to develop social anxiety too.

 Anxiety and other mental health problems tend to grow bigger and bigger when we try to ignore them.

In order to manage your anxiety, you have to make peace with it.

 There are lots of ways to do this— talk about your emotions, use CBT to understand them, express your emotions in any way that's easiest.

Most of all, don't try to avoid your anxiety or be afraid of experiencing it!

 You'll never completely get rid of anxiety, and that's okay!

You can learn how to not be scared of it so that it doesn't get too bad or take over your life!

DEALING WITH OUR EMOTIONS

Being a teen girl is tough. Being an autistic teen is exponentially tougher. Our teen years are a time when we're trying to figure out who we are. This is hard for everyone, but especially hard if you're autistic. Our bodies are going through physical changes and we are dealing with peer pressure, social media, boys, bullies and schoolwork, all while trying to manage our sensory issues and our social communication difficulties so that we can fit in and conform to society's narrow definition of "normal." It's like being on an emotional rollercoaster of highs and lows. Although it can sometimes feel as if your emotions are controlling you, there are techniques you can use to help you to identify and deal with your emotions. Below is a four-step approach that you can use:

1. **Name what you're feeling.** Try to identify the emotion you're feeling. It may help to think about the situation or event that triggered the feeling. For example, if you got a lower grade than you were expecting on the recent history test you spent all weekend studying for, you're probably feeling disappointed and frustrated. Naming the feeling helps to give you a sense of control. The more you practice identifying your emotions, the better you will get at recognizing the emotion that you're feeling.

2. **Accept what you're feeling.** Own your feelings. Remind yourself that it's all right for you to feel what you're feeling. Whether you're feeling anxious, sad, angry, stressed, disappointed,

embarrassed, excited, jealous or any other emotion, give yourself permission to embrace your feelings.

3. **Express your feelings.** The best way to manage your emotions is to express your feelings. This doesn't necessarily mean that you have to talk to someone, although talking to someone you trust may help. There are also other positive ways of expressing your feelings. For example, you could express your feelings by writing about them or drawing them in a journal, or you could go for a walk or jump up and down on your bed. Whatever outlet you choose, be sure that it doesn't injure you or anyone else.

4. **Practice self-love.** Pick a healthy way to take care of yourself. Do something that you enjoy and will make you feel better—for example, listening to music, cooking or baking, taking a warm bath or taking your dog for a walk.

Being in synch with your emotions will give you a sense of control. You will be in the driver's seat, instead of just being along for the ride.

DEPRESSION

There may be times when your emotions spiral out of control. Depression is common in teen girls and even more common in autistic teen girls. Depression is different from the normal mood fluctuations we experience as part of puberty and the social anxiety most autistic people suffer from. The main difference is that depression is characterized by a feeling of worthlessness and hopelessness.

Autistic people are more likely to experience depression. One of the main reasons autistic individuals suffer from depression is that we are frequently misunderstood, bullied and discriminated against. This can damage our self-esteem and make us feel bad about ourselves.

If you're having a difficult time deciding whether you're experiencing anxiety or depression, below are some of the symptoms of depression:

- continuous low mood and feeling of sadness
- feelings of hopelessness and pessimism
- feelings of worthlessness and helplessness
- finding no pleasure and enjoyment in life or the things you usually enjoy, including your intense interests
- decreased energy, and motivation, and an over-whelming sense of fatigue
- restlessness and irritability
- insomnia or oversleeping
- low appetite
- thoughts of harming yourself
- thoughts of death or suicide or suicide attempts.

After a particularly bad stretch of bullying at school, I fell into a short period of depression. I was overwhelmed by a sense of helplessness and a sense that I had to resign myself to always being rejected, mistreated and abused by my classmates. It was a dark and despairing time. I struggled to get out of bed, lost my appetite, was unable to sleep and felt listless and lethargic. I was a ghost of my former self. Depression is nothing to be ashamed of. If you're feeling depressed, it's really important to tell your parents, school counselor or anyone else you trust and to ask for help.

SELF-HARM

According to SelfharmUK, about 13% of young people self-harm. If you're feeling particularly low, you might self-harm in order to cope with distressing thoughts or feelings, painful memories or overwhelming situations and experiences. Some teenagers use self-harming as a way of expressing something that they have trouble putting into words, as a way of turning invisible thoughts or feelings into something visible and as a way of turning emotional pain into physical pain. Self-harming may make you feel better in the short term, but it can be very dangerous and can make you feel much worse in the long term.

In order to stop self-harming, you will have to understand why you're hurting yourself. The more you understand about why you're hurting yourself, the better equipped you will be to make the changes needed to stop self-harming. In order to better understand why you hurt yourself, you may want to ask yourself the following questions:

- What caused you to hurt yourself the first time?

- What situations cause you to want to hurt yourself?
- How do you feel before you hurt yourself and after you hurt yourself?

Understanding your patterns of self-harm can help you to identify what is causing you to self-harm and to recognize when you feel the urge to self-harm. Once you identify your self-harm triggers, you will be in a better position to control your urge to hurt yourself. It may be that the urge to hurt yourself is triggered by a specific thought or feeling or finding yourself in a particular situation. If you're able to recognize your urges, you can take steps to reduce or stop self-harm and to explore healthier and safer ways of dealing with your emotions.

Reaching out for help can be scary, especially if you're worried that people will judge you. Remind yourself that everyone needs help and support at some point in their lives. I think it is actually really brave and courageous to ask for help. When you're ready to reach out for help, choose someone whom you trust to talk to about how you're feeling. This could be a family member, a teacher or a friend. You may also find it helpful to write a list of all the people and charities that you can go to for help when you're finding things particularly overwhelming and difficult. This list will help to remind you that you're not alone and that there are people who can help you.

Unfortunately, there is no magic cure or easy solution to stopping self-harming. You may find that you take two steps forward and one step back. If this happens to you, don't despair and don't give up. Remind yourself that you're not failing, you're simply on a mission that will have some successes and some setbacks, but what matters is that you're trying your best and eventually you'll succeed. Remember that you can accomplish anything you set your heart on achieving.

SUICIDE

Suicide is the act of intentionally taking your own life. Suicidal feelings can range from being preoccupied by abstract thoughts about ending your life, or feeling that people would be better off without you, to thinking about methods of suicide or making clear plans to take your own life. If you're feeling suicidal, you might be scared or confused by these feelings. Remember that you're not alone. Many people think about suicide at some point in their lifetime.

If you're feeling especially low and hopeless, you might find yourself thinking about suicide. Whether you are only thinking about it or actually considering a plan to end your life, these thoughts can be overwhelming, difficult to control and very frightening. If you're worried about acting on your suicidal thoughts, tell someone. Although it may seem scary, asking for help is the best thing you can do for yourself and your loved ones.

Instead of focusing on all the desperate negative thoughts that are overwhelming you, focus on believing that these dark feelings will not last forever and on how to get past this difficult time. I suggest that you focus on reasons to live, because the world is a much better place with you in it. You could do the following:

- Write a list of all the things you're looking forward to, whether it's seeing a loved one, catching up on the next episode of your favorite TV show, going to a music concert or celebrating a birthday.

- Make plans to do something you really enjoy in the near future. Your plans don't have to be elaborate and expensive. It could be something as simple as playing a video game or going to the cinema.

- Think of all the people who love you. No matter how terrible you're feeling, don't ever forget that your family and friends would be devastated without you. You matter. You're irreplaceable. Don't ever forget that.

Remember to be kind to yourself. Talk to yourself and treat yourself as if you were talking to a good friend you really care about. Do whatever you think might help you to banish the negative thoughts. Eat some chocolates, watch your favorite comedy, listen to uplifting music, draw or do anything else that you enjoy doing and that can distract you. It's also really important to remind yourself that you can get through this rough patch. Tell yourself that you can overcome these dark feelings.

Suicidal feelings can be overwhelming. It is common to feel as if you'll never be happy or hopeful again. But with the right support, the majority of people who have felt suicidal go on to live happy and fulfilling lives. The earlier you let someone know how you're feeling, the sooner you'll be able to get the support and help you need to overcome these feelings.

BUILDING RESILIENCE

Resilience is the ability to bounce back after a negative experience or setback. Autistic teen girls are very resilient. Although our negative experiences are unpleasant at the time we're going through them, they're also very useful in that they help to build our resilience. They also help to remind us to appreciate the good times we've had and the positives in our lives. Setbacks and disappointments will happen throughout our lives. Knowing that you will survive and will be okay in the end is empowering. In order to continue to build your resilience, below are some responses that you can use when you experience a disappointment or have a setback. Remind yourself of the following:

- How you feel right now is not how you'll feel later.

- It's normal to feel sad/upset/angry/frustrated/scared now, but these feelings will pass.

- The experience will make you stronger and wiser.

- You'll be proud of yourself for getting through a tough situation. Even if you initially fail or take two steps backwards, you'll be proud of the effort you made and of the fact that you didn't give up.

- You're not alone. Many other people have dealt with a similar situation or worse.

- There are people who want to help you if you need help. Asking for help is not a sign of weakness.

- Although it may not seem like it right now, there will be many happy and amazing moments in your life.

If you focus on repeating these positive thoughts to yourself, they will help you to put things into perspective and will help you to cope with whatever life throws at you. I've found that sometimes good things can come from horrible experiences. If I hadn't been mercilessly bullied, I wouldn't be writing this book. In many ways, I have my negative past experiences to thank for who I am today. And so do many other people. If Malala Yousafzai, the Pakistani activist who was shot in the head by a Taliban gunman when she was a schoolgirl, hadn't gone through that experience and resolved to continue to fight for female education, she wouldn't have become the Nobel Prize-winning worldwide human rights advocate that she is today.

Finding Your Fashion Style

There's a lot of pressure on girls to look a certain way, especially in the era of selfies and Instagram. As you've probably noticed, most teen girls put a lot of effort into their appearance. They may highlight their hair, wear makeup, paint their nails, wear jewelry and own a wide range of fashionable clothes and shoes. Each of which can be a very unpleasant sensory experience for someone with sensory sensitivities. Although there are days when I would love to wear the cute outfits worn by the female characters in TV shows such as *Gossip Girl*, *Pretty Little Liars*, *13 Reasons Why* and *Riverdale*, the reality is that my sensory sensitivities don't allow for this. If I were to wear one of those outfits, it would be sensory torture. I've found that it's more important to wear clothes that are comfy and don't cause discomfort or pain.

I vividly remember one instance when I wore something that caused me to be in agony. Whenever I wear tights, I always cut off the label and wear a cotton vest that I tuck underneath the tights to create a barrier between the waistband of my tights and my skin.

Unfortunately, one morning, I overslept and my normal routine got disrupted. It wasn't until I was on the subway that I realized that I had forgotten to cut the label off my school tights and that the tights and label were rubbing against the bare skin of my lower back. Over the course of the next 15 minutes, the pain became intolerable. It felt as if I had a tiny miner drilling into the base of my spine. It was excruciating! No amount of peer pressure to wear the latest fashions is worth that level of pain. It may be that your sensory processing disorder affects you differently and that you can tolerate a much wider selection of clothes. If so, count yourself lucky.

DEVELOPING YOUR OWN PERSONAL FASHION STYLE

Most neurotypical teen girls place a lot of importance on fashion and looking good from head to toe. Who can blame them? We're constantly bombarded with images, whether from Instagram, vloggers, films, TV shows, adverts or fashion magazines, that tell us how we should look and what we should wear. We're surrounded by images of perfect-looking models and perfect-looking celebrities who are impossibly thin and impossibly beautiful promoting the latest fashion trends. Although most neurotypical teen girls feel a lot of pressure to emulate these looks, thankfully most autistic girls aren't as easily swayed by peer pressure and fashion trends. Sometimes, however, our lack of interest in fashion can make us an easy target for mean girls to make fun of and ridicule.

Autistic teen girls are much more likely to dress for comfort and for our sensory sensitivities, which means that our clothes may not be very fashionable or trendy. If I could, I would live in baggy sweatpants and hoodies or, better yet, my flannel pajamas. But since some people will judge you on your appearance, and the way you dress can give people a negative impression, I make an effort. I don't want people to think that I don't care about how I look and I certainly don't want to attract unwanted negative attention to myself.

If you're looking for a style that works for you, I suggest that you start by identifying your style icon. Identify a TV or film character or a celebrity that dresses in a style you like. I love the way Cara Delevingne and Kristen Stewart dress—maybe because both have been described as high-fashion tomboys. Once you find your style, identify the pieces that you like and search for these staple pieces online. The great thing about shopping online is the wide choice. You can find almost any brand or item online. Even more importantly, shopping online allows you to avoid going to the mall (and all the sensory issues this entails). It's also really convenient; if you don't like the fit or material, it's really easy to exchange or return.

It may take you a while to find a shop or brand that sells clothes that you like and that you can also wear. I've had to return lots of items that I liked, because they turned out to be too itchy or too uncomfortable. If you find an item of clothing that you both love and can wear, I highly recommend that you buy two or three of them and, if available, buy the item in different colors. I have a sweatshirt that's so perfect that I bought three of them.

Don't be afraid to create your own uniform. I've found a simple and timeless style that works for me. I gravitate towards black, which means 99% of my clothes are black. I wear black Levi high-waisted slim jeans that I wash over and over until they're really soft. I wear a selection of classic sweatshirts that are made of high-quality ultra-soft cotton. I've found that sweatshirts are more versatile than people give them credit for. I have some that have a weave that makes them look like sweaters and some that have a lace overlay, making them trendier than just a plain sweatshirt. Since I get cold very easily, I always layer with a cotton or velvet cardigan, hoodie or a blazer. My outfit is versatile and classic enough that I can wear it to school and also wear it to my after-school job.

I want to emphasize that what you wear doesn't define who you are. There are things that are so much more important, such as being kind, generous, thoughtful, accepting and forgiving. You probably have most of these traits in abundance. Having said that, sometimes autistic teen girls are judged by their peers for what they wear and can be mercilessly teased and bullied for it. You may want to dress in a way that helps you to blend in, so that instead of focusing on what you're wearing, people can focus on your positive qualities, such as your sense of humor, intelligence, honesty and trustworthiness.

THE IMPORTANCE OF WEARING A BRA

Some autistic girls resist wearing a bra. You may find them uncomfortable and perceive them as unnecessary.

However, there are times when we have to conform to society's dress code, especially when it comes to modesty. Your body is private, so you don't want people being able to see your nipples or breasts through your clothes. Not wearing a bra will also draw public attention from your classmates and others. This extra attention could result in teasing, hurtful comments and even sexual harassment.

If you dislike going to the mall, I suggest that you ask your mom to buy a selection of bras online. It is usually easy to return any that you don't like. First, you will need to find your bra size. Bra sizes have two parts: a number and a letter. In order to find your bra size, start by getting a tape measure and measuring around your ribs below your breasts to get your rib size in inches. You will now need to convert that number into a bra band size. If the number is even, add 4 and that's your band size. For example, if you measure 30 inches around, your band size will be 34. If the number is odd, add 5 and that's your band size. For example, if you measure 31 inches around, your band will be 36.

To calculate your cup size (the size of your breasts), measure loosely around the biggest part of your chest and subtract your band size from that number. For example, if your band size is 34 and your cup measurement is 36, the difference is 2 inches. Cup sizes are measured in letters. Below is the conversion:

- 1-inch difference = A cup size
- 2-inch difference = B cup size
- 3-inch difference = C cup size
- 4-inch difference = D cup size

- 5-inch difference = DD cup size.

Now that you have your bra size (which is made up of a number and a letter, such as 34B), think about what style of bra is best for you. Bras come in lots of different styles, fabrics and colors. Take your breast size into consideration and how much support you will need. I suggest soft-cup bras. They are soft and flexible, which makes them the most comfortable to wear. Sports bras provide more support and can be just as comfortable. Another option is an underwired bra. They have a curved wire sewn into the fabric along the bottom of each cup. The added structure provides more support. However, they can be uncomfortable. I avoid underwired bras. I dislike the sensation of the wire, especially when I slouch and can feel it sticking into me.

When selecting a bra, also factor in your sensory issues. You'll probably find pure cotton more comfortable than synthetic materials. Also consider whether you would prefer the fastener in the back or in the front. Having the fastener in the front is easier if you have motor coordination difficulties. Bras come in lots of bright colors and fun patterns. However, bright colors and patterns can be very noticeable if worn under light-colored tops. Be sure to buy at least one plain bra that matches your skin tone so that your bra doesn't show through your light-colored clothes.

Once you have a bra in your size that you like, you may need to make some adjustments. Most bras have two or three hook-and-loop fastenings at the back. Decide how tight or loose you want the band to fit around your rib cage by hooking the clasps on the tightest or loosest setting. You may also want to adjust the shoulder straps to make them longer or shorter. Also, don't forget to take it off before you go to bed— thankfully, there's no need to wear a bra when we go to sleep. Believe it or not, it took me a while to realize this and I actually slept with mine on for almost a year!

MAKEUP: TO WEAR OR NOT WEAR

Many autistic teen girls don't wear makeup for a variety of reasons. One reason is that we tend to go against the grain. We pay less attention to trends than our neurotypical classmates. Another reason is that our sensory sensitivities to smells, textures, creams and powders can make the prospect of putting these products on our face very unappealing. Most of my neurotypical classmates started wearing makeup when they were around 12 years old. At the time, I wasn't remotely interested. Also, my face was so sensitive that I wouldn't have been able to tolerate wearing makeup.

About two years ago, I slowly started experimenting with makeup. I started watching YouTube makeup tutorials from makeup artists and beauty vloggers like Wayne Goss and Jeffree Star. I also began researching different makeup brands online and reading product reviews and recommendations. Surprisingly, I find watching beauty vlogger tutorials and product reviews relaxing and a good way to combat stress and intrusive thoughts. My first purchase was a basic makeup kit from Bobbi Brown that was subtle, neutral and natural. From there, I gradually built up my collection and my tolerance. Before I knew it, I found that I really enjoyed experimenting with different products and looks.

Just to be clear, I'm by no means trying to encourage you to wear makeup. It's very much a personal choice. But if the reason you don't wear makeup is sensory intolerance, don't completely rule it out. As I've gotten older, I've found that some of my sensory intolerances have improved, which has allowed me to try things that were previously completely off limits. Having said that, wearing makeup isn't for everyone. Don't feel pressured to look a certain way. How you look and whether or not you wear makeup doesn't define your worth as a girl.

9

Socializing and Making Friends

Although most autistic teens need a lot of time to themselves, we also want to feel a sense of belonging and to feel accepted by our classmates. Friendships are important because they offer companionship, can be a great source of support and can protect us against bullies. Most autistic teens find making and keeping friends challenging. Whether we're outgoing or we're shy, socializing and developing friendships doesn't come naturally to us. It doesn't help that many neurotypical kids can sense that we're a bit different, even if they don't know why. To them, we may seem "odd" or may come across as being a loner. It also doesn't help that as we get older, socializing becomes much more complicated. The teen social scene involves lots of conflict and drama, especially as teens begin to develop crushes and begin dating. Teens also start to become more independent. Most neurotypical teens choose to spend less time with their family and more time with their friends. Overnight, friendships become so much more important.

DON'T TRY TO BE SOMEONE YOU'RE NOT

Feeling different to everyone else or feeling left out is a horrible feeling. It can be very tempting to try to be like everyone else and try to fit into other people's expectations so that you can make friends. You may even feel the pressure to behave very differently to how you normally behave. Masking (pretending to be someone you're not) is exhausting and will eventually make you feel bad about yourself. People may also see through your pretense. They may notice that you're not who you're trying to be and may become suspicious of you. Instead of trying to be someone you're not, focus on finding friends who you have something in common with and who will like you for who you are.

USEFUL CONVERSATION STARTERS

Sometimes, it can be hard to know how to start a conversation or what to talk about. I find that having a few pre-prepared conversation starters can help to avoid awkward silences. If you find yourself in a situation where you're at a loss as to what to talk about, here is a list of topics you might want to use to start a conversation:

- What are you doing this weekend?

- Have you seen a good movie recently?

- Do you have a pet?

- Which songs or music artists are you listening to?

A great way to start a conversation is to ask someone a question and to listen to their answer. Remember that most people like to be asked about themselves and like to be asked what they think about something.

FINDING LIKE-MINDED FRIENDS

If you're having trouble finding classmates who you have something in common with, join a school club that interests you. This will give you the perfect opportunity to meet other teens who like the same things as you. Instead of the usual chit chat, you'll be able to talk about your shared interest. This will make it so much easier to socialize. If there isn't a club you're interested in at your school, ask your school if you can start your own club. Since I love math, I once started a math club.

You might find a wider range of interests served by clubs outside of school. When I was younger, I joined a local archaeology club, which meant I got to meet lots of kids who were as interested in history as I was. My sister joined a Sunday choir group, which means she has met lots of kids who love to sing. Whether you're interested in dance, drama, chess, robotics, baking, reading or anything else, find a club you can join where you will meet kids who share your interest. Once you find other kids who share your interest, it will be much easier to socialize and develop these relationships into friendships.

BE DISCIPLINED IN YOUR CONVERSATION SKILLS

Sometimes, we can get really enthusiastic about what we're talking about, especially when it relates to our intense interest. Always make a point of showing an interest in what other people are saying. Be careful not to hijack the conversation so that you only talk about your own interests. If you show an interest in others, they are more likely to be interested in what you have to say and to be more interested in hanging out with you. Also, try to be open-minded about looking beyond your own interests. Everyone needs balance, and not everyone will have the same interests as you. Try to find out about their interests and talk about other topics as well as your own interests. I have a friend at school who loves comic books. I've tried to learn a bit about different comic books so that I can talk to him about something he finds interesting. Much to my surprise, I have found that I enjoy reading the backstories of the Marvel characters. You may find that you end up learning about topics you wouldn't otherwise have explored and that you might really enjoy.

EDIT WHAT YOU SAY ALOUD

When chatting and interacting with others, be careful not to say anything which might be perceived as rude or inappropriate. If you dislike someone's new haircut or you think someone smells bad, keep it to yourself. No good will come from being too honest. You will only end up hurting someone's feelings and causing people to get upset with you. In situations like this, it's better to edit what you say aloud. As the saying goes, if you don't have anything nice to say, don't say anything. These are good words to live by.

BEING A GOOD FRIEND

Being a good friend essentially means that you treat people the way you would like them to treat you. When thinking about how to treat other people, put yourself in their shoes. Ask yourself how you would feel in their situation. If you would feel upset or uncomfortable, then you shouldn't put other people in that situation. Friendship is a two-way street. In other words, both people have to work to make it a good friendship.

No one is perfect. Everyone makes mistakes. The important thing is to learn from your mistakes, so that you don't keep repeating them. If you have upset or offended friends or classmates in the past, try to learn from the experience. If you're worried about unintentionally doing or saying something that may upset your friends, I recommend that you are open and honest about this. Here are some suggestions:

- If you have upset someone in the past because you regularly interrupted them, you could say:

  "I have been known to get excited and to unintentionally interrupt people. I am working on not doing this. If I interrupt you while you're talking, can you let me know?"

- If you sometimes talk too loudly, you could say:

  "Sometimes, I talk too loudly. I'm not always aware that I'm being too loud. Can you let me know if I talk too loudly?"

- If you sometimes unintentionally say something hurtful to someone, you could say:

  "Occasionally, I say something I really wish I hadn't said. If this happens, could you please let me know? I would never want to deliberately hurt your feelings."

Your friends are more likely to be understanding and forgiving if they know that you're trying to address any behavior they find a bit annoying or upsetting.

Another way to be a good friend is to be loyal and caring. Little gestures that let your friends know you care can mean a lot to someone—for example, saving a friend a seat at the lunch table, sticking up for your friends if they're being teased and sending a friend copies of your class notes if she or he missed a day of school. Remember the golden rule: treat your friends the way you would like to be treated.

WORK ON UNDERSTANDING
HOW OTHER PEOPLE FEEL

Seeing things from someone else's point of view and understanding how someone else is feeling are important social skills. In order to be a good friend, it helps to know what your friends may be feeling. The best way to understand how other people may be feeling is to imagine how you would feel in the same situation. Having said that, trying to understand how other people feel is incredibly difficult, so be patient with yourself.

When I was 12, I was friends with a girl called Charlotte. A month before her birthday, she told me that she was certain her parents would forget her birthday and that no one would get her a birthday cake. Everyone repeatedly reassured her that she shouldn't worry about her parents and friends forgetting her birthday. But she wouldn't listen. Charlotte was insistent that her birthday would go unnoticed and uncelebrated. On the day of her birthday, I brought a chocolate birthday cake to school. I thought I was being a good friend and that surprising her with a cake would make her happy. Boy, was I wrong! When I excitedly presented her with the birthday cake, she told me she hated chocolate and stormed off. I was really confused! It wasn't until I got older that I realized that what Charlotte had really wanted was sympathy and attention. It was never about whether her parents would forget her birthday or about being worried that she wouldn't get a birthday cake; Charlotte was feeling insecure and wanted her friends to reassure her that she was important to them. She used her birthday story as a way of gaining attention and sympathy from her friends. By giving her a birthday cake, I took away her ability to continue to be the center of attention. I mention this experience to give you an idea of how hard it can be to understand other people. If someone had brought a chocolate cake to school for me, I would have been ecstatic. As you can see, social situations are rarely that straightforward. People are complicated.

ASK FRIENDS FOR SUPPORT

You may be reluctant to ask others for help, especially if you've been disappointed or let down by friends in the past. However, true friends can be a great source of support. Being open about some of your challenges will help them to understand you better. If they understand why you may behave and react differently to other kids, they will be in a much better position to help and support you. If you feel comfortable enough doing so, tell your friends about some of the challenges you face that may affect the way you behave or respond to certain situations. For example, many autistic people have a hard time with changes to their routine. I find that knowing exactly what to expect really helps to reduce my anxiety. The problem with rigidly relying on our routine is that we find it very distressing if our routine unexpectedly changes. Most people wouldn't understand this because they don't mind being spontaneous. When I was 12, I always sat in the same seat on the school bus. One day, a new girl decided to sit in my seat. Although it sounds silly, not being able to sit in my usual seat was extraordinarily unsettling. It almost caused me to have a panic attack! Worrying about where I would sit the next day was all I could think about. Luckily, I was able to confide in a friend, who helped to make sure that I was able to reclaim my usual bus seat the following day. Knowing that I could count on her if a similar situation happened in the future helped me to feel less anxious at school. If your friends know about your particular challenges, they will be in a better position to understand and support you.

AVOID GOSSIP

Teen girls love to gossip. I'm the first to admit that sensational gossip can be really entertaining and amusing. However, it's always at someone else's expense. Gossip is a form of bullying. It's hurtful and cruel, especially if it embarrasses or humiliates the person being gossiped about. Gossip can also ruin someone's reputation. I know how damaging gossip can be. When I was 14, two bullies at my school started spreading false rumors about me. They told my classmates that I was a "psycho" and that I belonged in a mental institution. Before long, my whole class was gossiping about me. They would whisper to each other as I walked down the hallway. I even had people I'd never spoken to ask me about my latest suicide attempt. No one seemed to care that there was no truth to the rumors and gossip. My classmates probably thought it was harmless fun. Although it was amusing to them, being on the receiving end was devastating. Since I know how horrible it feels to be gossiped and lied about, I avoid gossiping about other people. My general rule is that if I wouldn't want to repeat the rumor in front of the person that the rumor is about, or if I wouldn't want someone to say those things about me, I don't take part in the conversation. I will either change the subject or excuse myself. Don't forget that someone who gossips and says unkind things about another person is also very likely to spread gossip about you. The best way to avoid getting caught up in gossip and teen drama is to avoid people who gossip. Instead, hang out with people who are kind, sincere and caring towards others.

APOLOGIZE WHEN YOU MAKE A MISTAKE

We all make mistakes. It is very likely that there will come a time when you make a mistake and will have to apologize. For example, you may have forgotten a friend's birthday or you may have accidentally told someone something private that you promised your friend you wouldn't repeat. If you make a mistake and need to apologize, below are some suggestions as to how to do so:

- Apologize to your friend in person. Be sincere when you say you're sorry.

- Don't make excuses for your behavior. If you try to make excuses for what you did, it could seem as if you aren't truly sorry.

- Do something nice to make things up to your friend. For example, you can bring them some cookies or write them a note.

If your friend doesn't forgive you, you may have to give your friend some time to cool down. The best thing is to give them some breathing space. Try approaching them in a few days to see if they're more open to accepting your apology.

AVOID TOXIC FRIENDSHIPS

Not all friendships are healthy. Some friendships can be toxic. Instead of making you feel good about yourself, these friendships make you feel awful about yourself. These friendships are dangerous because they can wreck your sense of self-worth. Here are some signs of a toxic friendship:

- Your friend often makes you feel bad about yourself by being critical and saying mean things about you.

- Your friend needs constant praise, but never praises you back.

- Your friend behaves very differently when other people are around—she or he may even ignore you or be mean to you in front of other people.

- Your friend makes you feel guilty if you spend time with anyone else.

- You know that your friend is not very kind towards you, but you hope she or he will change.

- When you have confided something private to your friend, she or he has later used the information against you.

- Your friend is always in charge and rarely lets you have a say.

I have had a few toxic friendships. It's been my experience that these types of friendships initially start well. But for whatever reason, the friendship slowly and gradually becomes toxic. Sometimes it happens so gradually that you don't notice it happening. When I was 12, I was friends with a girl who frequently put me down and who would get really angry if I spent time with anyone else. Since I thought my other classmates weren't keen to be friends with me, I felt I had to stay friends with her. Although she was making me unhappy, I didn't want to end the friendship, because I was afraid of being friendless and alone. Eventually, I realized that it was better to be alone than to be around someone who was making me miserable. The funny thing is that as soon as I stopped hanging out with her, I was able to develop healthy friendships with other classmates.

DON'T FORCE YOURSELF TO SOCIALIZE IF YOU DON'T FEEL UP TO IT

Autistic people are very good at enjoying their own company. Most of us need a lot of time to ourselves. We need alone time to recharge our social batteries and to calm our overactive senses. Although there is a lot of pressure to socialize, sometimes the best thing you can do for yourself is to be by yourself. If you're not feeling up to it, don't force yourself to socialize. Well-meaning parents and family members may worry that you spend too much time alone and will try to encourage you to spend more time socializing. This is because most neurotypicals don't recognize the value of alone time. They associate spending lots of time alone as a sign that someone is depressed or anti-social. But this isn't always the case, especially not for autistic people. Whereas most neurotypical people get energized by being around other people, we get energized by spending time by ourselves. Most autistic people find socializing emotionally and physically draining. Spending time alone is the way we settle our minds and soothe our senses. Don't let anyone make you feel bad about needing alone time. Take care of yourself. Be kind to yourself. Love yourself. Be your own best friend.

10

Crushes and Dating

Crushes and dating are a natural part of growing up. If you haven't already, at some point you may develop romantic feelings towards a boy or a girl. You may find yourself becoming attracted to a classmate or someone you know. You may even develop intense feelings for a celebrity. From one day to the next, you're fascinated by someone. Just thinking about them may make you feel funny inside. You might even find yourself spending hours daydreaming about them and imagining what it would be like to be with them.

Entering the world of crushes, romantic relationships and dating is challenging for most teens, but it's especially challenging for autistic teen girls. The world of dating is complicated. There are so many unwritten rules and people rarely say what they mean. This makes it tricky for us to tell whether someone is interested in us. It also makes it tricky to know how to appropriately express our romantic interest in someone. If you come across too strong, you are in danger of being seen as desperate, whereas if you come across as being too distant, you are in danger of being seen as uninterested. Sometimes it can be hard to find the right balance.

RECOGNIZING ROMANTIC FEELINGS

Since many autistic people have difficulty recognizing their feelings, you may not realize that the sensation you're feeling is the feeling of being attracted to someone. If you have romantic feelings for someone, you may experience a tingly sensation or you might find that you are constantly thinking about the person and want to spend all your time with them.

When it comes to dating, neurotypical teens like to play it cool. But as you know, autistic teens are known for being honest and blunt. We're more likely to be open and uninhibited about expressing our romantic feelings for someone. However, appearing too keen and eager can be off-putting and can overwhelm the person you are trying to impress. Most neurotypical teens are reserved about openly expressing their romantic feelings, especially at the early stages of a romantic relationship. So be careful not to be too full-on. The fact that teens consciously dial down the way they express their romantic feelings makes it harder for us to work out how someone feels towards us. However, there are common signs that can indicate whether someone likes you. Below are some signs that a person may have romantic feelings towards you:

- The person acts a bit nervous around you.
- The person regularly smiles at you.
- The person does nice things for you (for example, regularly compliments you or gives you their coat to wear when it's cold outside).

- The person leans towards you (people lean towards people they like and away from people they dislike).

- The person frequently touches you (for example, puts their arm around you or puts their hand or arm on the small of your back to guide you).

- The person remembers what you tell them (a sign that they are being attentive).

- The person wants to be around you or always seems to be nearby.

- The person sends you text messages and promptly responds to your text messages.

If you notice that the person is showing some of the signs listed above, you will have to decide whether you feel the same way towards them and whether you would like to take the relationship to the next step.

ASKING SOMEONE OUT ON A DATE

If you have romantic feelings for someone, try to gauge how the person feels about you. Pay attention to how they behave. If the person displays the signs mentioned above, such as regularly smiling at you, complimenting you, making frequent physical contact and often texting you, they may be interested. On the other hand, if the person is inconsiderate, dismissive and unresponsive when you reach out, it's unlikely that they reciprocate your feelings. If this is the case, there is no point in asking the person out on a date. You deserve to date someone who will be kind and considerate and who thinks you're amazing.

Once you decide that the person you like may feel the same way about you, you may want to ask them out on a date. Asking someone out on a date is nerve-racking for everyone. After all, you don't know how the person you like will respond. But if you don't ask them, you will never know. Think about the best way to ask your romantic interest out on a date. Decide whether you want to ask them by text or in person. If you decide to ask in person, make sure you ask them when they are alone so that you have some privacy. Do not ask the person while they are around their group of friends, because you're likely to get interrupted. You could ask the person to meet you in the library before school. Don't be too pushy or aggressive. You may want to phrase it so that it comes across as laid-back and casual. For example, "Since we get along so well, would you like to go see a movie together this Friday?" If he or she says yes, you now have confirmation that they feel the same way towards you. You have both taken the first step towards the start of a romantic relationship.

HANDLING REJECTION

Sometimes, someone who you may have strong romantic feelings for may not feel the same way about you. When someone doesn't return your feelings, the rejection can hurt. Remember that this is not a reflection on you. The two of you are simply not compatible. Although you may feel angry and upset, remind yourself that it isn't anyone's fault. In order to have a romantic relationship, both people need to feel the same way. It's important that you respect their decision. Keep in mind that sometimes someone will make up an excuse to try to spare your feelings, instead of being honest and telling you that they don't like you romantically. For example, the person may tell you that they are too busy to go out with you. Don't keep on asking the person on a date if they have already said no a few times. Don't try to persuade them to change their mind. Don't say nasty things about them. Instead, distract yourself. Redirect your focus and attention on your intense interests. This will help to take your mind off your hurt feelings.

TURNING SOMEONE DOWN

Sometimes, someone who you don't have romantic feelings towards may like you. Turning somebody down isn't easy. As awkward as it may feel to reject somebody, it's best to be honest. You shouldn't start a relationship that you don't want simply because you didn't have the nerve to speak up for yourself. Tell the person that you don't want to be their girlfriend. Remember to be respectful and kind, but firm.

HEALTHY AND RESPECTFUL
ROMANTIC RELATIONSHIPS

A healthy romantic relationship involves being with someone who respects, supports and trusts you, and who appreciates you for who you are. A good relationship is built on enjoying each other's company, having fun together, helping and supporting each other, being kind to each other, trusting each other and accepting each other's faults. One of the most important characteristics of a healthy relationship is having the freedom to make your own choices and not feeling pressured into doing things that make you uncomfortable, especially when it comes to physical intimacy (such as touching, cuddling and kissing) and having sex.

SEX EDUCATION

It may be that you have pieced together information you know about sex from what your parents have told you, what you have overheard from other kids at school and from your school sex education class. You may have already discovered that some people find it difficult or embarrassing to talk about sex. They may feel that sex is private and personal, and they may feel uncomfortable talking about it. You shouldn't let this prevent you from educating yourself so that you can make informed decisions about sex and your body. The best way to learn about puberty, sexuality and sex is through books. Unlike people, books don't get flustered or embarrassed. Books include detailed information and can include useful illustrations. They can be revisited and re-read. The more knowledge you have, the better prepared you will be. Unfortunately, girls who are sheltered from learning about sex are much more vulnerable and susceptible to being taken advantage of and being manipulated into doing something they may later regret. The more information you have about sex and how to take care of your body, the more empowered you will be to make decisions about sex. In the "Where to Find More Information" section of this book, I recommend some books for you to read.

YOUR BODY BELONGS TO YOU

Your body is yours. It belongs to you. No one has the right to make you do anything to your body that you don't want them to. No one has the right to touch your body, unless you want them to. If you don't want to be touched or to be touched in a particular area, don't be afraid to say "No." It's your body and your choice as to what you do and don't want to do. Don't worry about disappointing or offending someone; if the person really cares about you, they will respect your wishes.

CONSENT AND SAFETY

If you decide that you want to have a sexual relationship or are ready to have sexual intercourse, it is important that both you and your partner consent to this and that you are both practicing safe sex. **Consent** means that both of you want to have sex and are not being forced or pressured into doing so. **Practicing safe sex** means that you are both being careful to protect against an unwanted pregnancy and against sexually transmitted infections.

Sometimes, you may feel indirect pressure to have a sexual relationship because your classmates may be having sex or because you may believe that it will help you to fit in and make you more popular at school. Keep in mind that teens often exaggerate or lie about their sex life. Don't believe everything you hear! It's important to respect yourself and to make the decision that feels right for you.

If you're wondering whether or not to have sexual intercourse with someone, ask yourself if your reason for doing so is one of the following. If it is, you should seriously reconsider because you may regret it later.

- Because your boyfriend or girlfriend is pressuring you.

- Because you're afraid your boyfriend or girlfriend will dump you.

- Because you feel uncomfortable saying "No."

- Because you're afraid of hurting the other person's feelings.

- Because you think it will make you popular.

- Because you think everyone is doing it and you don't want to be left out.

- Because it will prove how much you love someone.

- Because you think it will make the person fall in love with you.

Some boys see sex in a different way to most girls. Some may see it as a challenge, game or popularity contest. This will motivate them to say things to you that they don't mean in order to try to deceive you into doing something sexual. At one school I went to, the boys had a score card and ranked themselves on the number of girls they had sex with. These boys would pretend to like a girl so that they could have sex with her. Immediately afterwards, they would ghost her and bad-mouth her to their friends. These types of boys are likely to take advantage of girls they perceive as vulnerable and trusting. Since autistic teen girls are especially vulnerable to being tricked and taken advantage of by these types of boys, it's important for you to be wary of any boy who is pressuring you to send him nude pictures or who is pressuring you to do other sexual things you aren't comfortable doing. The odds are that someone who is pressuring you in this way does not have good intentions towards you.

SEXUAL ABUSE

Unfortunately, it is common for girls to be sexually abused. If someone tries to kiss you, touch you or hold you in a way that you don't want them to, or tries to force you to kiss them, touch them or hold them in a way you don't want to, it is **sexual abuse** and is illegal. If someone makes you have sexual intercourse when you don't want to, it is called **rape**. Rape is a serious crime.

Girls who are sexually abused often feel that it is their fault. Many feel guilty and wonder if they did something to cause them to be abused. This is not true!

If you've been abused, it's not your fault. If you are ever abused or you think you have been sexually abused, you must tell a trusted adult right away. Although it may be scary and embarrassing, you must tell someone. Don't suffer in silence. You deserve to be comforted, cared for and reassured that you are not to blame.

KNOWING WHEN TO MOVE ON

Ending a relationship is never easy. But if a relationship isn't working, it's best to admit that you're in a relationship that isn't quite right so that both of you can move on. The best way to break the news is to be honest. Don't be mean. Explain that you don't want to go out with them anymore. You could say something like "I liked it better when we were just friends" or "We don't seem to be getting along very well."

STAYING SINGLE IS FINE

Sometimes well-intentioned parents or family members pressure us to be "like the other kids." You may have family members who ask you if you have a crush on someone or whether you are dating someone. You may feel that there is an expectation that you should be dating because many of your classmates have boyfriends or girlfriends. What parents may not understand is that sometimes being part of a social group or being "like the other kids" is highly over-rated. Parents don't seem to realize that many of our classmates behave in a way that no caring parent would approve of. My 16-year-old classmates regularly get drunk, smoke, take drugs, send nude pictures of themselves and have sex, often indiscriminately. I don't want to appear judgmental, but since I'm not interested in participating in risky behavior that could jeopardize my future, I prefer to keep to myself outside of school. At school, I am friendly to my classmates, but since I don't view their behavior as "fun" or something I want to take part in, I prefer to stand up to the pressure to be like the other kids. I would rather stay true to myself than take part in this type of behavior. If you feel uncomfortable having to take part in certain behaviors so that you "fit in," don't be afraid to stand your ground. Don't compromise who you are so that you can be like everyone else. You don't have to conform to other people's ideas and expectations. Remember we were made to stand out. We walk to the beat of a different drum.

11

Gender Identity: Androgyny, Gender Fluidity and Transgender Girls

Autistic girls can find traditional gender roles confusing. Although there are girly autistic girls, many of us tend to lean towards being **androgynous** (gender-neutral). This can make others uncomfortable. In general, the world likes to divide people into two clean categories: male and female. This binary system classifies gender into two distinct genders that are unchangeable, extreme opposites and completely disconnected from each other. In reality, gender is fluid and lies on a continuum that isn't confined to two genders. This explains why many autistic individuals (both male and female) consider themselves to be **non-binary** (not exclusively masculine or feminine, but rather a combination of both).

There have been times in my life when I have been feminine and times when I've been androgynous. When I was around four, I was obsessed with the Disney princesses. I insisted on wearing a garish polyester

Cinderella ball gown. I was willing to endure the sensory discomfort caused by the scratchy dress because I desperately wanted to look like a magical princess. As I got older, I became much more practical about my appearance and my clothes. I chose clothes for utility and comfort. I also chose clothes that did not cause sensory overloads. I went through a phase when I bought superhero T-shirts from the boys' department. I found that boys' clothes were more comfortable and wearable. I also preferred their color palettes of gray, navy blue and black, to the usual sparkly pinks and purples that dominated the girls' clothes.

At a time when the other girls in my class were wearing makeup and were obsessed with getting their hair highlighted and nails painted, I was a tomboy. I wore my hair in a messy ponytail, wore gender-neutral clothes and wasn't remotely interested in emulating the models featured in the fashion magazines. This caused a few classmates to accuse me of being a lesbian—an accusation many autistic girls hear.

These days, I consider myself to be a **cis girl** (I identify with the female gender I was born with). I have created a style of my own that works for me. I wear makeup. I straighten my hair and wear it down (I wasn't able to do this before because my sensory sensitivities meant my hair hurt the back of my neck). When it comes to my clothes, I have an informal uniform. I wear black high-waisted Levi skinny jeans and a variety of soft, cotton sweatshirts and hoodies, and I wear the same black-and-white Adidas Superstars every day (I tend to do that with shoes). On rare occasions, I will wear a dress, but I never, ever wear high-heeled shoes.

If you're more androgynous than girly, you've probably felt some pressure to conform and to be more feminine. Whether the pressure comes from the media, your classmates, your friends or family members, remember that it's okay for you to be yourself. Find a style that works for you and make it your signature look.

TRANSGENDER GIRLS

There are some autistic boys who feel that they should have been born a girl. Boys (and girls) who don't identify with the gender of their birth are called **transgender** or **trans**. Trans is an umbrella term. As with any attempt to define a group of people, it encompasses a broad range of expressions and behaviors. Many transgender people may identify as female or male or may feel that neither label fits them. They may identify as non-binary, **gender-fluid** (someone who experiences shifts and changes in gender identity) or **genderqueer** (someone who identifies as something other than male or female, and generally does not believe in binary gender). Some transgender people choose to remain in their assigned gender, others choose to undergo hormonal treatment, and some choose to fully transition by having gender reassignment surgery (gender confirmation surgery).

Transgender and Autism

In the last few years, there have been lots of studies researching why autistic children appear to have higher rates of **gender dysphoria** (the clinical term for the distress caused by a mismatch between someone's biological sex and their gender identity). Some of these studies have concluded that instead of having gender dysphoria, some autistic children develop a "special interest" in their gender identity that can be confused for gender dysphoria. These researchers believe that autistic children trying to make sense of why they feel so different to everyone else sometimes mistakenly attribute their difference to gender dysphoria rather than to their autism. Since some of these studies are flawed, we're still a long way from having a conclusive answer. I think that it's possible that the frequency of gender dysphoria among neurotypical children and autistic children may be similar. However, since neurotypical children are more likely to conform to social norms, they may be more willing to suppress their gender dysphoria, whereas autistic children are not as deterred by having to conform to societal norms.

Coming Out

If you're certain or fairly certain you're trans, you may decide to **come out** (to tell people that you're trans) so that you can begin your transition from a boy to a girl. Coming out may feel really daunting and terrifying. There is no easy way or right way to tell someone you're trans. Remember that every trans person has felt the way you're feeling, yet with the right information, advice and support, they accomplished what they once thought they would never be able to.

Before you come out to anyone else, you should first come out to yourself. Coming out to yourself requires self-exploration, a process of getting to understand yourself better. You will need to be honest with yourself about how you feel and will need to reflect on who you want to be. This will include acknowledging your own gender identity and deciding how you want to express it. You may decide to conceal your gender identity from others or you may decide to tell everyone. There is no hurry—go at your own pace. There is no ideal time to come out. Trans people come out at all stages of their lives. Coming out is a different experience for everyone. You should make the decision that feels right for you. You should feel confident in your decision, rather than feeling that you have to come out. For some trans girls that may mean that they will publicly live as their true selves, whereas for other trans girls it may mean only coming out to themselves. Remember that the decision is not an all-or-nothing decision—many trans people come out to varying degrees. It may be that you choose to come out only to your family and close friends.

If you decide that you want to come out publicly, you will probably want to tell your parents and your closest friend or friends first. You should prepare yourself for the possibility that you may not initially receive a positive response. If that happens, don't despair! You may have blindsided them and caught them by surprise. It can often take people time to process information that they weren't expecting and for them to show their support. Some people may be shocked and confused, and may not have an accurate understanding of what it is to be trans, which will mean that you will need to educate them. On the other hand, you may find that coming out as a trans girl goes more smoothly than you expected. It may be that your news actually doesn't come as a surprise to your parents and close friends and that you merely confirmed what they already suspected.

Dealing with Parents and Family

The hardest part of coming out is telling your parents and family, especially if your family has very traditional views of gender roles and identity. It is possible that your news gets a negative response. For one thing, your parents may struggle to come to terms with such a big change. They may really struggle to accept that they're losing their son. In some ways, it may feel like a death to them. They may go through a series of emotions ranging from denial to shock, confusion, anger and grief. Some parents may react badly and may need time to accept the new you. It's important for you to be patient and that you emphasize to your family that you're not really changing—on the contrary, you're embracing who you really are and who you've always been. If your parents and family are having a particularly difficult time accepting your true gender identity, you may want to recommend that they contact an organization that supports trans parents, such as Mermaids, and that they meet other trans families who can provide them with support and who can answer any questions they may have.

Transitioning

If you decide that coming out is the right decision for you, the next step is to decide how you will transition from being a boy to being a girl. Transitioning is a process that takes time. It's a good idea to start gradually by making minor changes, so that you can determine how you feel. Having others perceive you as the gender you identify with can be challenging at first. You will probably want to start by picking a female name and asking people to call you by your new name. Be patient. When you first start using a new name or female pronouns (she/her), you may frequently have to remind people to call you by your new name.

The best way to prepare to transition from being a boy to a girl is to be very observant of how teen girls look, behave and speak. Identify a teen girl who is physically similar to you and observe her. Observe how she looks, such as the clothes and accessories she wears and how she wears her hair. Observe how she behaves, such as her mannerisms and the way she speaks. The secret to passing as a trans girl is to project confidence. If you walk and act confidently, you are less likely to receive unwanted attention. You may be tempted to dress overly feminine, but you may want to dress to complement your body shape. If you have a more masculine physique, try dressing in clothes that girls with that body shape are likely to wear. If you would like a more female physique, consider wearing a bra with breast forms that are appropriate for your body type. Realistic-looking breast forms can be expensive, but www.nicolajane.com sells a selection that are reasonably priced.

I'm a trans girl. This means I wasn't physically born a girl. But I've known that I'm a girl for as long as I can remember. A couple of years ago I started transitioning my body to fit the gender I identify with. This included dressing in more feminine clothes and wearing cute makeup!

I'm non-binary. This means I don't feel comfortable identifying fully as a girl or a boy. My pronouns are they/them. I often like to dress in more feminine clothes, but that doesn't mean I want to identify or be addressed as a girl.

I'm a cis girl. This means I identify with the gender I was born with. I don't really act or dress in a feminine way. This doesn't mean I don't feel like I'm a girl, though!

All of our experiences and feelings about our genders are personal, varied and all valid! There isn't a correct way to act or feel about your gender, what matters is that your identity is respected!

One easy way of appearing more feminine is to have long hair. A fringe can also help you to appear more feminine. Another easy way to appear more feminine is to wear makeup. I suggest that you start gradually and wear subtle makeup that looks natural. Start with mascara and a tinted lip balm. If you have facial hair that is barely visible, it is probably best to leave it alone. If, on the other hand, you have visible facial hair and your sensory sensitivities can tolerate it, you may want to try using hair removal cream or wax. You may also want to soften and raise the pitch of your voice, so that you sound more feminine.

Public Bathrooms

Deciding which bathroom to use is a difficult issue that all trans people face. Trans young people should be able to use the bathroom of the gender they identify with. In other words, trans girls should be able to use the girls' bathrooms. However, the prospect of using the girls' bathrooms may make you feel vulnerable. You may be worried that you could be confronted. You may also be worried that you could be subjected to transphobic bullying. Some trans students find the prospect of using the bathroom at school so overwhelming that they refuse to. I have a friend who is a trans girl who used to reduce her water intake and would wait until she got home to go to the bathroom. However, she now comfortably uses the girls' bathrooms at school. If you're not using the bathroom at school, it's important that you try to address this by coming up with a solution that works for you.

In an ideal world, all places would have mixed-gender or gender-neutral single occupancy bathrooms. But mixed-gender bathrooms are not often readily available. If you're uncomfortable or feel unsafe using the girls' bathrooms, you may consider using the disabled bathrooms instead. Some trans youth prefer to use the disabled bathrooms over using the bathroom of the gender of their birth. However, many only do so as a last resort. Some trans young people are concerned about depriving disabled people of using the bathrooms that were designed for them. And some resent having to use the disabled bathrooms because their trans status is not a disability. Whatever decision you make, it's important that you feel safe using the bathroom you intend to use.

Sexual Orientation and Relationships

Sexual orientation (who you are attracted to) is completely unrelated to your gender identity. You can be trans and straight, trans and gay, trans and bisexual, asexual, or anything else. Whether you identify as straight, gay, bisexual or queer, knowing how and when to tell someone you're interested in about your trans status makes dating more complicated. However complicated, it's always best to be honest and upfront with anyone who you would like a physical relationship with.

After you transition, you may use another word to describe your sexuality. For example, a trans girl who is attracted to boys might describe herself as a straight girl, although previously she may have been seen by society as a gay boy.

Identifying Positively as Autistic Trans

Living as a trans girl has its challenges. A good place for you to start identifying positively as trans is to be true to yourself and to remain positive about who you really are. Just because you're autistic trans doesn't mean that you don't have the same opportunities and the same prospects as everyone else. Autistic trans people are usually successful in their chosen careers, have good friends, fall in love and have loving relationships with their family, just like everyone else.

12

How to Survive School

School can be a nightmare for autistic kids. Trying to survive in an environment that is blind to many of our challenges can feel like an uphill struggle... It can almost feel as if somebody deliberately set out to design schools to be as difficult as possible for autistic students. Even autistic kids who have mild sensory sensitivities to loud noise, bright lights, bustling crowds and other sensory information are almost certain to become anxious and overwhelmed by the fluorescent lights, kids yelling, the crowded hallways, the strong, overpowering smells of the cafeteria, science labs and changing rooms, and the many other day-to-day school sensory experiences.

Our biggest challenge is that the school environment is fundamentally a social environment. In order to be successful at school, students must be able to interact, socialize and communicate well with others. Since we may not understand some of the "rules" that govern social situations, we're always struggling to catch up. Just as we begin to master the social rules, the social rules change. It doesn't help that people often say something and then get upset with you for failing to realize that they actually meant something entirely different. The anxiety that comes with being out of synch with neurotypicals and our school environment can prevent us from learning and can negatively affect our academic performance.

TIPS ON HOW TO SURVIVE SCHOOL

Although the school environment is not an ideal place for autistic students, there are ways to make our school experience more pleasant and less stressful. Below are some tips that I use to help me to survive and overcome some of the main challenges that we face at school.

Managing an Overstimulating Sensory Environment

One of the main reasons that autistic teens find the school environment so traumatic is that it's the worst combination of noise, crowds, lights and smells. You may get really anxious about:

- going to the noisy, crowded, brightly lit, smelly cafeteria

- walking down a bustling hallway between lessons

- attending whole-school assemblies that are loud and crowded

- trying to access your locker when the hallway is jam-packed with students.

The difference between an autistic person doing great in school and doing badly can be down to just a few simple adjustments that a school could make to help our autistic brains navigate a neurotypical environment.

Having our senses overstimulated can leave us over-whelmed and struggling to cope.

TIP

Small changes can have a huge impact on making your school environment less stressful. There are lots of ways your school can help to manage and reduce the overstimulating sensory environment. For example, if you're anxious about having to push through a crowded hallway to get to your next lesson, ask if you can be allowed to leave your lessons five minutes early when the hallway will be empty and quiet. If you frequently feel anxious in class, ask if your school will give you a "time out" card that you can use to leave the classroom and go somewhere quiet when you feel anxious and overwhelmed. Don't feel shy about raising sensory issues with your school. You're unlikely to be the first person at your school who has felt overwhelmed by the overstimulating sensory environment. You may be surprised at some of the solutions that your school proposes. If not, don't hesitate to come up with some of your own proposals.

Handling Changes in Schedules and Routines

Autistic kids love the predictability and certainty of schedules and routines. Routines are a great way to manage the anxiety that comes from living in a world that is not designed for us. Knowing exactly what to expect gives us the time we need to mentally prepare. When our school schedule or routine unexpectedly changes, it can throw us off balance. It can feel as if you're being made to walk down a plank and forced to jump into the ocean, even though you can't swim.

Last September, I started at a new school—a stressful experience for anyone, but especially for someone who's autistic. In order to cope in a new and foreign environment, I was relying heavily on my class schedule and the peace of mind that comes from knowing what to expect next. On my first week at the school, I arrived to what I believed would be a physics lesson, only to be informed that our afternoon classes had been cancelled and that, instead, my entire year group would be taking part in team-building activities. Within minutes, I found myself in a crowded and unfamiliar hall being blindfolded and made to do lots of physical activities that involved trusting strangers. The activities quickly descended into chaos, including lots of shouting, shoving, nudging, jostling, prodding, elbowing and collisions. It was one of the worst sensory experiences of my life! I don't know how I managed to keep my composure. By the end of the activity, I had several bruises and was almost catatonic. Not having been given advance notice of a major change to my schedule really unsettled me. Knowing that I couldn't rely on the certainty of my school timetable meant that I was in constant fear that at any moment I could find myself having to do some other horrific sensory activity.

TIP

The best way to avoid being unsettled by unexpected changes to your school schedule or routine is to ask your teachers to inform you in advance of any changes. Being given a few days to mentally prepare for any changes to your timetable will ensure that you aren't caught off guard. I find that knowing what to expect really helps to reduce my anxiety. Being given advance notice of any changes to your routine also gives you the opportunity to have some input in shaping the activity so that the school can modify the activity to make it more accessible for you. Don't forget to also have this request included in your Individual Education Plan (IEP).

Executive Functioning Challenges

Executive functioning is the ability to plan. These skills allow us to manage our time effectively, memorize facts, solve multi-step problems, understand what we read, organize our thoughts in writing, manage our homework and school projects, study for tests and much, much more. These skills are the bedrock of what is needed to succeed in school. Executive functioning is a major challenge for almost all autistic people. If you have difficulty getting organized, such as doing homework, finishing projects and remembering things, you may have executive functioning issues.

Below are some of the most common signs that you may have executive functioning issues (since ADHD is a problem with executive function, many of the signs are the same as the signs of ADHD). These signs include having difficulty:

- organizing your thoughts
- concentrating and maintaining focus
- organizing, planning and prioritizing tasks
- starting and/or completing tasks
- switching focus from one task to another
- following directions or a sequence of steps
- managing your time
- keeping track of your belongings.

TIPS

The best way to address executive functioning challenges is to put measures in place that will help you to organize yourself. Below are some of the tips and tricks I use to help me to succeed in school.

Color Code

I've found that one of the best ways to help ensure that I keep track of which book I need for which lesson is to use a color-coding system. Start off by color-coding your timetable. Assign a different color to each subject. Get some stickers with corresponding colors. For each subject, match the color you assigned on the timetable to the textbook and equipment. For example, if you assigned green to English, stick a green sticker on the spine of your English textbook and on your English folder. If you need to bring two items to your English class, write "2" next to "English" on your timetable. This will remind you to take two items to your English class. From now on, when you go to your locker to get your English books, all you'll need to do is find the two items with a green sticker.

Always Use a Checklist
The best way to avoid forgetting which books to take home and which books to take to school is to use a checklist. You may prefer to use a checklist app on your smartphone. The trick is to keep a list of all the items you need to remember to bring home that particular day and a list of all the items you need to remember to take to school that morning. Before you leave home or school, go through each item on the list to make certain that it's in your bag.

Break Down a Task into Smaller Sub-Tasks

Breaking down a task into smaller tasks makes it less daunting and reduces the risk that you will procrastinate. Whatever your goal, the first step should be to break it down into smaller, more manageable parts. For example, if you have to do an art project for homework, you may want to break it down into the following parts:

- **Step 1:** Decide what your art project will be.

- **Step 2:** Make a list of all the art materials that you'll need.

- **Step 3:** Gather all the materials and, if necessary, purchase any materials you need.

- **Step 4:** Schedule a time and select a place to do your art project.

- **Step 5:** Begin working on your project.

Planning is a great way to feel in control. By breaking up the task into small manageable pieces, you avoid getting overwhelmed and giving up before you've even begun.

Get Duplicates

If you are constantly forgetting items you need at home or at school, you may want to consider getting two sets of everything—one set that you keep at school and one set that you keep at home. I've found it's easy to buy copies of school textbooks on Amazon (you may even be able to buy previously owned textbooks). This approach also has the added benefit of making your school backpack so much lighter.

Get into a Routine

Since we have difficulty with time management, the best way to ensure that you have enough time to do your homework is to get into the habit and self-discipline of a routine. If you always do your homework at a set time, you'll be less likely to keep putting it off or do it at random times.

Learn to Prioritize

One of the trickiest aspects of high school is knowing how to prioritize your homework. Identifying which homework is due first and which homework will take the longest can be difficult. It can also be difficult to know how much to focus on each subject. It's tempting to focus on studying the subjects we like or are good at and to neglect the subjects that we dislike or find challenging. You may want to try using a homework student planner app or ask your teacher to help you.

Find the Right Work Environment

Since we have trouble focusing and can get easily distracted, it's important that you do your homework in an environment that is free from noise and distractions. Put your phone away. Switch off the TV. Declutter your desk. Create a calming and quiet environment where you can concentrate and focus on your schoolwork.

Although it may seem daunting, by putting a few organizational measures in place, you can significantly improve your executive function skills.

Socializing Challenges

Autistic teen girls struggle to socialize and "fit in." We may be able to cope with one-on-one interactions, but socializing with groups of people can be very overwhelming. Teen conversations and banter have a fast pace and back-and-forth momentum that can be difficult to follow. I always struggle to know when to interject and what to say. I always seem to be out of synch with my classmates.

TIP

Ultimately, all you can do is your best. Try not to be too hard on yourself. I've often found that schools assume that every student wants to have friends. Although this may be true for most, I actually like my own company. I'd rather be alone than be pressured into being friends with someone simply for appearance's sake and to avoid being judged. The problem with being forced into a friendship is that I was often pushed into being "friends" with people who weren't very nice. Don't feel pressured to be friends with someone you don't like or who makes you feel bad about yourself.

The best way to survive the social challenges faced by most autistic teen girls is to be selective about who you are friends with. It has been my experience that students who are "different" in some way are much more empathetic, compassionate and kind. I have a friend who was born with a facial difference, another who has cerebral palsy (a movement disorder) and two friends who are trans. They're all really amazing. They're the most non-judgmental, accepting and understanding kids I've met.

Intolerance of Autistic Behavior

Some teachers are confused by autistic girls, because our demeanor and behavior may not match up with their expectations of what autism is. These teachers may doubt that you're actually autistic or may quickly forget, because you don't behave in a stereotypically autistic way. Since our autistic characteristics aren't openly visible and in full view, it's easy for teachers to overlook us, especially since many autistic teen girls are model students. These teachers often place neurotypical expectations on you. They will pressure you to "fit in" and be more like the other kids. They'll expect you to get on with things, even if you're overwhelmed by being in an overstimulating sensory environment. I've found that classroom teachers who lack empathy towards their autistic students usually have little or no autism training. Their lack of knowledge prevents them from knowing how to understand, support and be sympathetic towards us.

TIP

If you have a teacher who doesn't seem to know much about autism, it may help to give them an article on autism in girls. I recommend nasen's "Girls and Autism: Flying Under the Radar." You can download a PDF version of the article off the Internet (www.nasen.org.uk/resources/resources.girls-and-autism-flying-under-the-radar.html). The article will give your classroom teacher a brief overview of the challenges you face. A little targeted knowledge should put your teacher in a better position to support, understand and be empathetic towards you.

Coping with Unstructured Breaks

Unstructured school breaks are a nightmare! If you don't have any friends at school or you prefer to be alone, not knowing what to do with yourself during unstructured break times can be very distressing. To make matters worse, since unstructured break times tend to be unsupervised, we're also much more susceptible to being bullied during break times.

TIP

I've found that the best way to cope with unstructured school breaks is to fill the time with an activity I enjoy. Since I find the hustle and bustle of the school day overwhelming, I like to use my school breaks to do something that calms and soothes me. I go to the library—a quiet and calm place where I can unwind and relax. You don't necessarily have to read a book. If you're not in the mood to read, you could do other relaxing activities, such as origami, drawing or playing solitaire.

Coping with Inconsistent
Rules and Expectations

Autistic kids love consistency. We don't like being uncertain of what to do and what is expected of us. Unfortunately, schools aren't always consistent with their rules and expectations. You may have one teacher who expects students to raise their hand in class before being allowed to answer a question and have another teacher who encourages students to shout out their answers. Inconsistent rules can be really confusing! My sister is always complaining about a teacher who has class favorites who get preferential treatment. This teacher once told my sister's best friend that she loved her necklace. This teacher noticed that my sister was also wearing a necklace, except instead of admiring her necklace, the teacher gave my sister a detention for wearing jewelry in school. My sister was really confused. She was also really upset at being treated unfairly. However, when my sister told the teacher this, the teacher gave her another detention for being argumentative.

Many autistic kids have a strong sense of justice and sense of right and wrong. When teachers apply rules inconsistently, we find the inconsistency not only confusing but also unjust and unfair. Yet teachers are rarely receptive to being told this. Unfortunately, autistic kids often get in trouble for informing teachers that they're applying their rules inconsistently. Although we're pointing out the truth, our message is rarely well received. We're more likely to be accused of being disrespectful and rude.

TIP

I've found that the best way to cope with inconsistent rules and expectations is to keep a log of the teachers who apply the rules inconsistently and list the rules that this teacher applies. This will help you to remember the different expectations that each teacher has. You also have to reconcile yourself to the fact that teachers are human and that life isn't fair. A teacher is never going to appreciate being told that they're being unfair. They will perceive your comment as a criticism and will think you're trying to undermine their authority. Sometimes, you just have to be satisfied with the knowledge that you know your teacher is in the wrong.

Coping with Teamwork and Collaboration

Autistic students can find teamwork and collaboration very challenging. I've been put in teams with students who refused to collaborate. They claimed to be too busy to be involved and so I was abandoned to do the project on my own. On one occasion, I spent days working on a group geography project that I was especially proud of. My teacher gave the project an A+, but gave us an F for teamwork. This teacher expected me to convince my team members to pull their weight, something I'm not capable of doing. I'm not a confrontational person and don't have the communication skills to persuade four uncooperative neurotypical teens to collaborate. On other occasions, I've worked on group projects with bossy and assertive team members who don't let you contribute. Every time you try, they ignore and dismiss you.

TIP

If you know in advance that you will be assigned a team project, I recommend that you tell your teacher that you find the social dynamics of working in a team challenging. Ask the teacher if they would be willing to allow you to give them a list of people who you would prefer to work with, and of people who you would prefer to avoid. Being on a team with students who are collaborative and respectful of each other will make the experience so much more pleasant.

Coping with Class Participation

Schools are obsessed with class participation. Whether I feel comfortable participating in class has a lot to do with my teacher and the dynamics of the class. Have you ever been in a situation where you're sitting in class and the teacher asks a question? You're prepared. You've done the reading and homework and you know the correct answer. As your eager classmates energetically raise their hands, you try to do the same, but something prevents you. You hear students blurting out answers, you listen to them engage in lively discussions, and while you would love to participate and engage, you can't. Unfortunately, if I'm having a bad sensory overload day or I'm particularly anxious, I'm in no state to be called on in class. I'm likely to freeze and become tongue-tied. The annoying thing is that I will have been paying attention to the lesson and will even know the answer, but being called on heightens my anxiety so much that I'm unable to respond. To make matters worse, all the teacher sees is someone who is so disengaged that they can't be bothered to participate. They don't see the battle that is going on inside my head.

> **TIP**
>
> One way to reduce the anxiety of being called on is to have a flag system. For example, if you're feeling particularly anxious, place a bright pink Post-it note on the corner of your desk to signal to your teachers to give you a break from being called on. Your school and teachers may be able to propose other solutions that allow you to build your confidence so that you will eventually feel safe enough to answer questions and contribute to class discussions.

Fine Motor Skill Difficulties

Many autistic teens have difficulty with their fine motor skills. Fine motor skills involve the ability to make small, precise movements with our fingers and hands. These small movements play an important role in whether we succeed in school. We rely on our fine motor skills to write, draw, type and to manipulate small objects (for example, to adjust a microscope in biology class or to use a calculator, compass and protractor in math class). Our poor fine motor skills explain why many of us still struggle to do things that most teens take for granted, such as manipulating buttons and zips, taking the lid off a water bottle, cutting our food and tying our shoelaces. When I was younger, I was always in trouble with my PE teachers. Although I tried my best to get dressed into my PE kit as quickly as possible, inevitably I was always last. I really struggled with buttons, zips and shoelaces. Instead of being understanding, my PE teachers accused me of daydreaming and threatened to give me a detention.

TIP

I've found that the best way to deal with fine motor skill challenges is to be honest with your teachers about your difficulties. If you tell your art teacher that you need more time to complete your drawings or art projects, she or he may allow you to work on a project at home or to work on your art during your lunch break. Being understood and supported by your teachers, especially your art teachers, science teachers and PE teachers, will make a huge difference to your school day. Don't forget to also have this request included in your IEP.

General Motor Skill Difficulties

Many autistic teens also have difficulty with their general motor skills. General motor skills involve the movement and coordination of our arms, legs and other large body parts. These movements involve big actions, such as walking, running, riding a bike and swimming. It's very common for autistic kids to be clumsy and uncoordinated. This can make PE lessons and school sports days a humiliating experience. Whereas all the other kids could effortlessly run or catch and throw a ball, I was an epic disaster. You could rely on me to be the slowest runner and to never, ever catch the ball. As you would expect, I was always the last member of a team to be picked. When I was eight, two kids cried when they realized I was on their team. They told me that since I was on their team, we were certain to be last in every event. PE lessons and school athletic events have been some of my most mortifying and embarrassing experiences.

TIP

The best way to deal with general motor skill challenges is to make your school aware of your difficulties. The most important people to tell are your PE teachers. They have the power to make your PE lessons fun or to make them a miserable experience. Be honest. Ask for their help and support. Tell them that you're trying your best and explain how embarrassing and demoralizing it can be to have to work so much harder at physical tasks that seem to come effortlessly to others. To be honest, from the age of ten, I started skipping sports day. The experience was too soul destroying. Instead, my mom and I would do something fun like go to the cinema. Don't forget to also have this request included in your IEP.

Changing-Room Challenges

Changing for PE or swimming lessons in front of other teen girls is a horrible experience. Setting aside the stressful social dynamics of girls gossiping and the non-stop chatter of girls catching up with each other, changing rooms are an assault on the senses. The smells of sweaty clothes and stinky shoes, deodorants, shampoos, hairsprays, makeup and perfume mingling in an unventilated room with the flickering and humming of fluorescent light beaming down on you can be overwhelming.

TIP

If you find the school changing room really overwhelming, ask your school to make some minor changes to make the environment less distressing for you. One option could be to be allowed to change somewhere else or allowing you to wear your PE outfit to school so that you don't have to change. The important thing is not to suffer in silence. Your school may be able to come up with a solution that helps to reduce your anxiety. Don't forget to also have this request included in your IEP.

School Cafeteria Challenges

In high school, most cafeterias are large, rowdy, bustling places. They are also one of the main places where students socialize. As if this weren't bad enough, the smells of the different foods can be overpowering.

I found the large high school cafeteria environment so overwhelming that I avoided going. I often went the whole school day without eating anything. I don't recommend it!

TIP

If you find the high school cafeteria environment too much to handle, you may want to ask your school if you can bring your own lunch and if you can eat it in a quieter and more relaxing location. Don't forget to also have this request included in your IEP.

School Uniform Challenges

If you go to a school that has a school uniform, you may struggle with sensory issues caused by the fabrics and textures rubbing against your skin. I had to wear a uniform that had an itchy wooly sweater and a scratchy polyester shirt and tie. The shirt rubbed against my neck, which was not only very distracting but also painful.

TIP

If you explain that your uniform is causing your sensory discomfort, your school may give you some leeway. Your school may allow you to substitute some of the uniform items with similar-looking items that don't cause you discomfort, such as replacing polyester shirts with organic cotton shirts.

KNOWING WHEN TO MOVE TO A DIFFERENT SCHOOL

Autistic kids are constantly expected to change and adapt to fit into the world, a world that wasn't built for us. In order for schools to really support their autistic students, they must be willing to meet us halfway by making some changes so that the school environment will be more manageable for us. Although autism awareness is crucial, the most important factor in determining whether we have a positive and successful school experience hinges on a school's willingness to adjust their approaches, support services, expectations and environment to allow us to fulfil our potential. Helping us to achieve our potential doesn't involve big, burdensome changes. Small changes can make a huge difference—for example, giving us a "time out" card that we can use to go somewhere quiet when we feel anxious and overwhelmed.

Unfortunately, a few schools just don't seem to be willing to put in the effort. They see us as problems and drains on their time and resources. Staying at a school that is unwilling to support you is a recipe for disaster. It will eventually wreck your physical, mental and emotional wellbeing. I know dozens of autistic kids who were so traumatized by their school experience that they resorted to self-harming, became deeply depressed and even attempted suicide. Sometimes the best thing you can do is cut your losses and walk away, no matter how unjust and unfair. You deserve to be in a school environment where you're understood and supported. You deserve to be in a school environment that helps you to be the best version of yourself.

THE BENEFITS OF HOME EDUCATION

Home education can provide a safe and secure place for us to learn in the way that we learn best: away from the overstimulating sensory environment and bullying of school. I was home-educated for six months and absolutely loved it! Below are some of the benefits of being home-educated:

- **One-to-one attention.** Being home-educated gives you the freedom and flexibility to tailor your education to your specific needs and interests. It allows you to set the pace of your learning. I was able to gallop ahead in math and the sciences in a way I wouldn't have been able to at school. I was also able to spend more time on my weaker areas, such as foreign languages.

- **Less pressure.** Studying and learning in the comfort of your home allows you to relax and be yourself, free of all the pressure to conform, socialize and cope with an overstimulating sensory school environment. I found that I was able to learn so much more easily and efficiently.

- **Enjoyment of learning.** Being outside the stressful school environment can rekindle your love of learning. You can also explore areas that genuinely interest you. I studied subjects not usually taught at school, such as psychology.

- **Free from bullying.** A huge benefit of being home-educated is that you're no longer at the mercy of school bullies who seem to have a talent for finding autistic kids to torture. Feeling safe and being free from abuse is liberating. It allows you to be happy and to feel positive about yourself.

- **Confidence and self-esteem.** Having a positive learning experience helps your confidence and self-esteem to flourish. Instead of constantly being made to feel inferior to our classmates and having our difficulties and challenges be the main focus, we're able to concentrate on developing our strengths, talents, abilities and interests. We are set up to succeed, instead of constantly being set up to fail.

Home education isn't for everyone. It's a big change to the traditional school environment. Below are some of the drawbacks of being home-educated:

- **Loss of income.** One of the major drawbacks of home education is that it usually requires a parent to give up their job. This could have a huge impact on your family's financial situation.

- **Expensive.** Home-educating can be expensive. The cost of textbooks, writing materials, science materials, art supplies, musical instruments and other school supplies quickly adds up.

- **Lack of specialist knowledge.** The parent responsible for your education may feel out of their depth. My mom wasn't able to teach me physics, chemistry or advanced math.

- **Potential isolation.** Being home-educated can be socially isolating. It takes more effort to organize social interactions.

- **No school reports.** Since you won't get school reports, it may be more difficult to apply to summer programs or to university. The process of finding someone unrelated to you to write a reference on your behalf can be more complicated.

Home education may seem like a drastic decision. However, if you're being bullied or if you're finding school life impossible, it's worth considering, even if only for a short while. No decision has to be permanent. If you're suffering in school, it's important to prioritize what's best for your mental, physical and emotional wellbeing.

SURVIVING TOXIC TEACHERS

There are some teachers who dislike kids who behave differently and who learn in different ways. These teachers have a one-size-fits-all approach to teaching that is rigid and inflexible. They begrudge making accommodations and adjustments for our sensory processing sensitivities, our anxiety or our learning differences. I suspect they view it as a form of preferential treatment that is unfair to the other students. Whether consciously or subconsciously, these teachers allow our classmates to make fun of us or to exclude us. I refer to these teachers—teachers who seem to go out of their way to embarrass, demean, shame and belittle us—as **toxic teachers**. Unfortunately, I've had more than my fair share of toxic teachers.

I had one particularly toxic teacher who repeatedly refused to make accommodations and adjustments for my sensory processing sensitivities, dyslexia and dyspraxia. Instead, she created a really challenging and hostile classroom environment for me. For starters, she assigned me a seat where I couldn't see the board. It took months of requests, emails and several parent meetings for her to finally move me to a different seat. In class, she regularly embarrassed and humiliated me in front of my classmates. She also regularly changed the format of her lesson to involve physical activities (such as running in and out of the classroom with our chairs and throwing objects across the classroom), despite knowing that the unexpected change and loud, frenzied, chaotic classroom environment would distress me.

Worse still, she used a form of gaslighting. She used psychological manipulation to make me question whether I was at fault and whether I deserved her scorn. Since she was so pleasant to other students and was generally well liked, I was disoriented and confused by how she appeared to be understanding and supportive of everyone, except for me. Had I done something to deserve it? Was I to blame? Eventually, her disdain for me began to affect the way she graded my homework and exams. She claimed that I was struggling with the content of her class and convinced the deputy head at my school to force me to drop the subject. Suspicious of her claims, my parents arranged to have the class homework and exams reviewed and re-marked by other teachers specializing in the subject at other schools. They wanted a second opinion, especially since my own school had predicted me an A in the subject at the beginning of the school year. The teachers who reviewed my work concluded that my toxic teacher had been significantly under-grading my work and was misrepresenting my aptitude and ability in the subject. Whereas my toxic teacher consistently graded my work a D, the other teachers graded the same work an A+. One of the teachers who reviewed my work was so impressed with my essays and knowledge of the subject that she recommended I study the subject at a "top university" and pursue a career in it.

I mention this not to boast but to demonstrate the extent to which some toxic teachers will go to depict you in a way that serves their agenda, no matter how far they have to stray from the truth. When my parents learned of the magnitude of the deceit, they made a formal complaint of disability discrimination against my toxic teacher. They didn't want any other student with special educational needs to have to go through the torment, distress, suffering and anguish I had had to endure at her hands.

The problem with toxic teachers is that they destroy your confidence and self-esteem. They make you doubt yourself and can even make you doubt your own sanity. After all, why would a person who chose to be a teacher and to work with young people be so cruel and spiteful? It makes no sense! Toxic teachers can have a devastating effect on your mental health and emotional wellbeing. I began suffering from panic attacks; even the thought of having to go to my toxic teacher's class triggered one. It got to the point that I began having nightmares about having to go to her class! Unfortunately, the world is full of people who abuse their power. Bullies come in all shapes and sizes. If you come across a toxic teacher, don't let them make you doubt yourself and don't let them take away your confidence and self-esteem. The sweetest revenge is succeeding in spite of them.

13

Bullying

I've been bullied at school for most of my life. It's very likely that you've been bullied too. In the Annual Bullying Survey carried out by Ditch the Label in 2017, 75% of autistic students reported being bullied. I'm not going to sugar-coat it. By far the most unbearable and traumatic experiences I have had involve being ridiculed, mistreated, abused, ostracized and rejected at school by my classmates. If you've ever been bullied, you'll know that it's a *horrible* experience. Being bullied makes you feel alone and unlikeable. You may even feel that you're somehow to blame. Trust me when I tell you that this isn't true. No one deserves to be bullied.

WHAT IS BULLYING?

Bullying is when a person or group sets out to repeatedly hurt, intimidate, scare or humiliate someone whom they perceive as vulnerable. Bullying can take many different forms, including:

- being called names, being insulted or taunted

- being teased, ridiculed, embarrassed, put down or humiliated

- having false rumors spread about you

- being excluded from social groups or being ignored

- having your belongings taken or destroyed

- being threatened or intimidated

- having people make things up to get you into trouble

- being pushed, hit, kicked, pinched, slapped or physically hurt.

Schools will often deny that you're being bullied or will dismiss a bullying incident as a "misunderstanding." I've had teachers tell me that name-calling and insults were just teen banter. These teachers focus on blaming the target of bullying instead of addressing the behavior of the bullies. When I have complained about being called a "freak," "psycho," "weirdo" and other mean names, I've had teachers tell me that I can't take a joke and that my autism causes me to misinterpret teen banter. Sadly, directing the blame at us is common. These teachers will tell you that you're too sensitive and should develop a sense of humor. Don't listen to them. They're wrong!

If your school tries to brush off your bullying complaint as teen banter or as a joke or disagreement, remind them that bullying is distinguished from harmless banter by the following four factors:

1. The negative actions are repeated and are intended to cause the person humiliation, distress or harm.

2. There is an imbalance of power (in many instances, the bully is supported by classmates, whereas the target is alone or may have a very small social group).

3. The incidents are one-sided.

4. The target is negatively affected, whereas the bully is not.

One of the biggest misconceptions about bullies is that they have low self-esteem. I've found the complete opposite to be true. All of my many bullies have been popular and confident and have had high self-esteem. Many were also the teacher's pet and were exceptionally talented at manipulating teachers and staff into believing them. Many were also skilled at getting their friends to lie and cover for them. The combination of being well regarded by teachers, being popular and having friends who will lie on their behalf makes these bullies invincible.

WHY ME?

Bullies are experts at identifying vulnerable people to target. Since some of us prefer to be alone and can sometimes be isolated from our peers, we may lack the friendship groups that can protect us from being bullied. Bullies look for someone who is different and who they think won't stand up for themselves. It's tempting to blame yourself or your autism for being bullied, but bullies will use any "difference" as an excuse to target someone. I know people who were bullied for being too tall, for wearing a hearing aid, for being clever, for having a stutter, for wearing glasses, for having acne, for their weight, for their choice of backpack and for having a facial birthmark. In other words, they can target anybody for almost anything. I have met many young people who've been bullied. The one thing they all had in common is that they were kind, understanding and compassionate. Some of the most amazing people I've met have been bullied.

FROM ZERO TO SIXTY

One of the alarming aspects of bullying is that it can start off as a harmless incident and can quickly escalate to abuse. At one school I attended, a girl wore bulky orthopedic shoes. Her two best friends began to tease her about her ugly shoes. Eventually, these girls managed to involve other classmates in mocking her. Before long, her classmates started calling her cruel names. The taunts soon evolved into pushing, shoving, punching and hitting. As the bullying escalated, her friends began avoiding her so that they wouldn't be picked on for being friends with a girl who wore "Frankenstein shoes." That school year, she wasn't invited to a single birthday party. The girl started taking a book with her to the playground during recess because nobody wanted to talk to her or play with her. Even if some children would have liked to play with her, nobody dared to, because they were too afraid of the other children's reactions. The social isolation, physical abuse and endless taunts caused the girl to start having panic attacks at school and to become distressed about going to school. That girl was me and I was eight.

DEALING WITH YOUR SCHOOL

If you're very lucky, you go to a school where bullying is not tolerated. In an ideal world, every school would crack down on bullying by holding bullies accountable and by following their anti-bullying policies. I've only ever experienced this once, at a lovely primary (elementary) school that didn't stand for any intolerance or unkindness. It was a breath of fresh air to go to a school where I knew I would be safe from abuse. Sadly, my experience has been that many schools create a bullying culture by denying that any bullying is taking place.

A Word About Teachers

Teachers are often held in high esteem. People seem to forget that they're human. They can be flawed and have biases and prejudices, just like anyone else. Sometimes, it's not just your classmates who are bullies. Teachers and school staff can be bullies too. I've come across some really cruel teachers and school staff who have misused their authority to incite bullying. The ones who constantly belittle you in the classroom and make jokes at your expense. The type of teachers who pretend they don't hear the name-calling and insults that are directed at you, and go as far as to blame you if you're bullied, because they believe you brought it on yourself for not making more effort to fit in. Unfortunately, teachers can be close-minded and intolerant too. If you have teachers like this at your school, try your best to avoid them.

The Blame Game

We should never be blamed for being bullied. Much too often, schools play the blame game. Instead of focusing on addressing the bully's behavior and promoting a tolerant and accepting school environment, they blame us. I've had teachers tell me that I wouldn't be bullied if I tried harder to "fit in." These teachers worsen the bullying by shifting the focus on us and making it appear as if we're somehow at fault. Schools that blame the victim and expect you to hide your disability (in other words, pretend to be "normal") are helping to create a hostile school environment in which students who are different become easy targets. If your school blames you for being bullied, remind them that they need to redirect their focus from expecting you to change to teaching acceptance and tolerance and to holding the bullies accountable for their behavior.

Reconciliation Meetings

Some schools have an unofficial policy of requiring the bully and the target of bullying to attend a "reconciliation meeting" to set aside their differences. At one school I went to, they insisted that I attend a meeting with my bullies, something my anxiety and fear of the bullies prevented me from doing. Although my parents and I repeatedly explained to the school that this approach was not appropriate when dealing with an autistic student, the school refused to listen. A reconciliation meeting assumes that both parties have the same social and communication skills and that both have the ability to express themselves and to advocate for themselves. However, since autism is a social communication and interaction disability, the school is requiring the autistic student to do something that is the very basis of their disability. It is the equivalent of asking a blind person to see or a person in a wheelchair to walk. An autistic student has difficulty with communication at the best of times. Forcing a distressed autistic student to be in the same room with their bullies and expecting them to express themselves and defend themselves against students who are lying and being manipulative is going to cause them to "shut down," a survival tool we often use when we become too overwhelmed. If your school is insisting that you meet with your bullies, remind them that requiring you to attend such a meeting is discriminatory, because they are putting you in a situation where your autism disadvantages you.

Document, Document, Document

Since it's very common for schools to deny that you're being bullied, it will be up to you to provide your school with detailed information. This can be problematic for people who are autistic. We're not great at retelling events in chronological order. We're also not great at relating an event in its entirety. Instead of seeing the big picture, we focus on one or two details. For example, if a bully were to insult me, kick me and throw my schoolbook in the toilet, initially I may only mention that the bully kicked me (because the pain of being kicked caused me the most distress). It is only later that I might mention that the bully also insulted me and damaged by schoolbook. But by that point, the bullying incident may have already been investigated and dealt with. Most neurotypicals don't understand that we perceive and respond to experiences differently. It often takes us much longer to process and express our experiences. Due to our communication difficulties, we often struggle to describe a bullying incident effectively, especially since anxiety and distress decrease our ability to express ourselves. I've learned that the best way to ensure that I provide a detailed account of each bullying incident is for me to write it down. It gives me time to process my thoughts and emotions. I suggest you try this approach. Start by creating a template that includes the following prompts:

- the time, place and location where the incident occurred

- the names of the people involved

- the names of any witnesses

- what the bully said to you (including any insults, threats, etc.)
- what the bully did to you
- whether there have been any previous incidents
- how it made you feel
- the effect the bullying is having on you.

When describing the event, try to write your account of the event in the order that it happened. You may also want to create a drawing of the layout of your school and mark the areas where you were bullied (you may find that there are certain bullying hot spots). A detailed written description will make it easier for others to have a better understanding of what happened. Another benefit of writing down your account of what happened is that it removes the element of social interaction and communication at a time when you are feeling overwhelmed. I've been in situations where school staff have interrogated me about a bullying event in front of the bullies who were vehemently denying that they had done anything to me. I don't respond well to confrontations. Being a target of bullying is distressing enough as it is. This is only made worse if I have to endure being interrogated by school staff, while the bullies fake-cry and pretend to be sorry. If you are anything like me, you may actually shut down. When I get too overwhelmed, I withdraw and hide in my head. Unfortunately, this means that school staff often misinterpret my "shutdown." Since I appear distant, detached and non-verbal, school staff assume that I'm not upset or hurt by the bully's behavior, which causes them to be less caring and sympathetic towards me.

Believe it or not, there have been instances where the bullies have put on such a dramatic performance that the school staff focused on consoling them and were fooled into feeling bad for them! I say "fooled," because the bullies would later laugh about having tricked the school staff into feeling sorry for them.

STRATEGIES TO USE IF YOU'RE BEING BULLIED

If you're being bullied, there are tried and tested strategies that you can use and that may help. Below are ten strategies you can use if you're being bullied:

1. **Ignore the person who's bullying you.** Pretend not to hear the bully's words. No matter how tempting, try not to let the bully's words upset or anger you. Imagine that you're surrounded by a protective bubble and that the words bounce off the surface of the bubble before they reach you. Not responding or reacting when someone says or does something mean is often the most effective response to bullying. Most bullies are looking for a reaction. If you get angry or cry, it may encourage the bully to keep going. If you ignore the person who's bullying you, it's possible that the bully will realize that he or she isn't getting a response from you and will eventually stop.

2. **Tell the bully to stop.** Most bullies don't expect someone to stand up to them. They often target classmates who they believe can be easily

intimidated. In fact, bullies often rely on finding a target who won't say anything at all and who will suffer in silence. If you feel bold enough to do so, telling the bully to stop in a strong, assertive and confident voice could be very effective. If bullies know that they can't intimidate you, they are more likely to stop.

3. **Never suffer in silence.** Many people who are bullied don't tell anyone. You may feel that you're somehow to blame. You may also be embarrassed or worried that the bully will retaliate or that you won't be believed. The best way to stop the bullying is to report it. Without the intervention of an adult, bullying will often continue and can even escalate. Although it takes a lot of courage to report bullying, it is the best way to address the situation. Even if you don't want to report it, speak to somebody you trust—a parent, trusted teacher or another responsible adult. Don't suffer in silence or feel that you have to go through this ordeal alone, because you don't.

4. **Avoid bullying hot spots.** I have found that a lot of bullying takes place during unstructured and unsupervised social time and in unmonitored areas within school, such as the cafeteria, common areas, hallways, bathrooms, stairwells, playgrounds, changing rooms and on the school bus. Sometimes the best way to deter bullying is to avoid crossing paths with your bullies. During unsupervised school time, such as my hour-long lunch break, I would go to the library or the nurse's office (the only two places at school

where I felt safe). If you cannot avoid hot spots, buddy up with a friend, if possible.

5. **It's not your fault.** It's normal to blame yourself and to start to feel that it's your fault that you're being bullied, especially if it's happening repeatedly. If someone's being nasty, it can make you wonder whether you've done something wrong. You may even begin to believe that you deserve it. I've had to change schools three times, because of bullying. I reached a point where I began to think that there was something wrong with me and that I had to resign myself to always being abused and mistreated. But bullying is *never* your fault. No one should be bullied, no matter who they are, what they look like or whatever their culture, sexuality, race or religion.

6. **Find inspiring role models.** When I was being bullied, I found it comforting to read about celebrities who had been bullied at school. My favorite actress, Jennifer Lawrence, was bullied so badly that she had to switch schools several times. Taylor Swift was bullied for liking country music. Rihanna was bullied for her skin color. When you're being bullied, it can sometimes feel as if you're alone. You're not. I suggest that you Google some of your favorite musicians, actors or celebrities to see if they were bullied. It is very likely that you'll find that some of them were. Remind yourself that they once went through the same experience that you're going through and that they not only managed to overcome it but are now having the last laugh. Imagine

how the mean girls who relentlessly bullied Kate Middleton, the future queen of England, now feel about their behavior. I'm willing to bet they regret having bullied her so badly that she changed schools.

7. **Focus on a hobby.** Find a few after-school hobbies that you enjoy. It could be a sport, an art class, a cooking class, a book club or some other group activity. Not only will you have fun, but you'll also get to meet people outside of school who you could become friends with.

8. **Lean on an anti-bullying charity.** There are lots of anti-bullying charities that are there for you. You may find it helpful to look at their websites and to read some of their online resources. I found it comforting to read some of the stories of young people who had been bullied. It made me feel less alone. Some charities also have a helpline you can call. I have included information on some of these charities in the "Where to Find More Information" section at the back of the book.

9. **Consider moving to another school.** Sometimes the wisest thing you can do is to cut your losses. If you're at a school that condones bullying by pretending it isn't happening or by blaming you, you may be facing a battle you can't win. Ultimately, a school sets the tone for the way students treat each other. If a school is prepared to allow its vulnerable students to be mistreated and abused, it's unlikely to be an

environment where you're going to be supported and where you will flourish. Although it may seem daunting, consider moving to a different school. You deserve to have a happy school experience free from mistreatment and abuse.

10. **Is it a disability hate crime?** Some types of bullying are a crime. If you're being targeted because you're autistic, it's a disability hate crime. If you're being called derogatory names, are being threatened or are being physically abused, you may want to talk to your parents about filing a disability hate crime report at your local police station.

USING ASSERTIVE BODY LANGUAGE

Did you know that most communication is non-verbal? Body language tells us a lot about other people. People communicate more information through their body language than they do through words. Our body movement, facial expressions and tone of voice say more about us than the things we actually say. Since one of the main symptoms of autism is difficulty with communication, many of us struggle with using body language (such as our posture, gestures and facial expressions) as a form of communication. Many of us are unaware of the message that our body language is communicating to others. If you're trying not to be noticed and are looking at the ground a lot while darting into school, it can make you more noticeable. Others will perceive you as being vulnerable and timid. If, on the other hand, you walk into school holding your head high and with purpose, you'll project confidence. You may not feel very confident, but you'll certainly look it.

Since bullies are more likely to pick on people whose body language conveys a lack of confidence, here are a few things you can do to "stand tall" and appear more confident and in control to others (even if you don't feel this way):

- Keep your back straight.

- Hold your head high.

- Walk with purpose.

- Take a deep breath and relax your shoulders.

- Unfold your arms and try not to fidget.

- Hold eye contact (look at the bully's forehead or between their eyes).

- Use an assertive voice.

Practicing Assertiveness

Being assertive drastically reduces the odds of being bullied. However, practice is key, especially if using body language does not come naturally to you. Adopting a more assertive body language may feel very foreign to you and may not work immediately, but with practice and regular use it will make a huge difference to the way that your classmates perceive and treat you. Below are some exercises you can do with your parents, a sibling or a trusted friend to develop a more assertive body language.

- **Role play.** Team up with someone to role-play typical bullying scenarios. Get them to play the bully. Discuss what the bully might say and prepare an action plan. Practice your assertive response—for example, ignoring them or telling them to stop. You might want to role-play further responses to any comebacks you might get from the bully.

- **Mirror work.** Look at yourself in a full-length mirror. How are you standing? Are you hunched over? Are your arms folded? Are you biting your lip? Are you looking away? Practice the assertive body language that I outlined above. Once you're feeling confident (or if you don't have a full-length mirror), get a parent, sibling or trusted friend to mirror your body language. Try to judge whether they appear timid or assertive.

- **Eye contact.** Most autistic people have a difficult time with eye contact. Some of us even find it painful. Yet neurotypicals expect others to look them in the eye. They interpret lack of eye contact as a sign that you're being dishonest or that you're overly timid and shy. A key part of appearing assertive is to make eye contact. Since you might find this challenging, the key is to look at the bridge of the bully's nose, so that it appears that you're making eye contact.

Learning how to convey assertiveness through your body language will take practice, but conquering this skill is well worth the effort.

FRIENDS OR FRENEMIES?

How can you tell whether someone is a true friend? Since most autistic teen girls have difficulty interpreting social situations, we find it hard to predict other people's behavior. We also find it hard to interpret their body language and facial expressions to try to figure out what they're thinking or feeling. This makes it difficult for us to understand other people's intentions. Since we take friendships at face value and can be very trusting, it is easy for people with ulterior motives to take advantage of us.

At school, we are vulnerable to becoming targets of backhanded bullying, a situation where we are offered "friendship" by someone who intends to mislead us, or by a "friend" who intends to trick us into doing something absurd or inappropriate in order to make fun of us. When I was 12, a group of girls, who claimed to be my friends, insisted that I wear a panda onesie to the school Christmas dance. They told me that they would be wearing animal onesies too. I believed them. Luckily, my mom intervened and made me wear a party dress. When I got to the dance, the girls were wearing party dresses and were visibly disappointed that I hadn't come to the dance dressed like a panda. At that moment it dawned on me that they had been playing a cruel trick on me. Unfortunately, autistic girls find it hard to tell whether someone is being genuinely friendly or whether they are "winding us up." Sadly, some of us get tricked into doing things by our classmates in order to get us in trouble or to have a laugh at our expense. Remember that a true friend wouldn't want to embarrass you or hurt your feelings. A true friend also wouldn't pressure you into something you're not comfortable doing.

WHEN BULLYING WRECKS
YOUR PHYSICAL, EMOTIONAL
AND MENTAL HEALTH

Being bullied can turn your life upside down. I was once bullied so badly that it wrecked my physical, emotional and mental health. Two boys who had been threatening me for months finally put their plan to get me locked up in a "psych ward" into action. They falsely told several members of school staff that I was suicidal and made up many other alarming accusations to make me appear to be mentally unwell. They also spread false rumors about me around school. Overnight, I went from being the girl no one noticed to the girl everyone was talking about. Since the two boys were popular, many of their friends got involved in the bullying and in covering for them. Although I had text messages from classmates informing me of the things the boys were saying about my autism and learning differences, my school insisted that the boys were lovely "gentle boys" who would never bully anyone. I, on the other hand, was described as "having it in" for people by making bogus bullying claims, as having a false sense of reality and as being paranoid. When the bullying continued to escalate, my parents and I were repeatedly told that the bullying was simply "my perception." In other words, I was told I was imagining it. Eventually, I became so distressed about going to school that I began to suffer from crippling stomach aches, blinding headaches, insomnia, loss of appetite and panic attacks. At school, I was anxious and scared. I spent my free time hiding in the library or the medical center. Despite being at the top of my class, I began to miss weeks of school. I was overwhelmed by a feeling of helplessness and despair. Eventually, I was left with no option but to leave the school.

If you have ever felt like I did or are feeling that way now, I want you to know that you're not alone. Many people who have been bullied have felt this way too. It's important that you talk to someone you trust, so that you can begin to move forward. You may also want to consider getting some counseling or professional support to help you to overcome the trauma caused by being bullied. My bullying-related depression lifted as soon as I left the school and was no longer in a toxic environment. However, I was so traumatized by the experience that I was referred to a post-traumatic stress disorder (PTSD) specialist for counseling. My parents and I felt so strongly that no one else should have to go through what I did that we took the school to a disability tribunal (a type of court) for disability discrimination. Although I will always bear the scars from the bullying and the way the school treated me, I now know that if I can survive that experience, I can survive almost anything.

SEXUAL HARASSMENT

Another form of bullying that many girls experience is sexual harassment. Sexual harassment is very common in schools. **Sexual harassment** is defined as unwelcome words or conduct of a sexual nature that have the purpose or effect of creating an embarrassing, hostile, humiliating or offensive environment for the victim. It can take many forms, including being the target of sexual comments, jokes and teasing, and being the target of sexual rumors. It also includes being shown sexual or indecent photos and being touched, grabbed or pinched.

When I was 11, a group of girls targeted me because I didn't follow fashion trends, didn't wear makeup and wasn't interested in boys. It didn't take them long to start calling me a "lesbo" and a "dyke" and for them to spread a rumor that I liked girls, which caused many girls to avoid me. I was hurt and confused. I didn't understand why the girls were using these labels as insults and why they were making inaccurate assumptions about me based on my appearance.

As I've gotten older, I've had to put up with lots of unsavory behavior from the boys at my school. Sadly, I hear sexist, misogynistic language at school almost every day. In class, boys openly talk about girls' bodies and what they do to them. They frequently also talk about porn or watch it on their laptops. I try to ignore their behavior. However, I've found that sometimes it can stay with you and affect you more than you realize, especially since we're often expected to laugh it off or "get over it." Much too often, we feel pressured to excuse the behavior as "boys being boys" and as innocent banter, when it is actually sexual harassment. If you're a target of sexual comments, jokes and teasing or the target of sexual rumors, report the abuse to a teacher you trust or tell your parents. One of the reasons this behavior is so common and has become so normalized is because most girls have learned to accept the abuse and therefore don't report it. The more teen girls speak out and report the abuse, the less it will be allowed to go on!

GETTING YOUR LIFE BACK ON TRACK

Being bullied can knock your confidence and your sense of self-worth. Overcoming the trauma of being bullied is a hard thing to do. Building yourself back up will take time. One approach that really helped me was to use my bullying experience to help others who are being bullied. Wherever you live, the odds are that there's a local or national bullying charity or organization that you can become a part of. I did an online search for local anti-bullying charities and sent them an email asking how I could get involved. This led to being selected to serve on the 2018 Diana Award National Anti-Bullying Youth Board, where I represented thousands of anti-bullying ambassadors throughout the United Kingdom. It was a very empowering experience. It gave me a platform to help others by sharing my autism-related bullying experience. It also gave me an opportunity to become friends with an amazing group of kind and compassionate young people who had also been bullied and who also wanted to help to tackle bullying so that no one else suffered as they had done.

There are many ways you can help others. You could volunteer with an anti-bullying charity, set up a peer support group at your school or write a guest blog during Anti-Bullying Week. You may find that using your experience to help others helps you to regain control of your life again. I want you to know that although it may not feel like it, you won't feel broken forever. Little by little, you'll find that your life is back on track and that you're back to being yourself.

14

Co-occurring Conditions

It is very unusual for someone to only be autistic. Most autistic people have one or more other conditions, such as Tourette syndrome and epilepsy. These are referred to as co-occurring conditions (or co-morbid conditions). As soon as you are diagnosed as being autistic, schools should automatically consider whether you could also have any of the common co-occurring conditions that can affect your ability to succeed in school. Sadly, schools often fail to make the connection, which means that many kids are left to struggle unnecessarily at a time when they need the help the most. I don't want that to happen to you, so please consider whether any of the symptoms of common co-occurring conditions listed below describe you and your experiences.

In my case, in addition to being autistic, I also have ADHD, anxiety, dyslexia, dyspraxia and hypermobility. Each of these conditions is challenging on its own. Having a combination of these conditions takes the challenges I face to a whole different universe! The sooner you're diagnosed and the challenges you face are identified, the sooner you can get the additional support and understanding you'll need to better manage these conditions.

ADHD IN AUTISTIC GIRLS

Many people still believe **ADHD** is a condition that only affects boys. When most people think of ADHD, they imagine a boy who can't sit still and who acts impulsively. Girls can have ADHD too. But most girls with ADHD act very differently to the way most boys do. Girls are more likely to have **inattentive ADHD** or ADD (a form of ADHD that involves difficulties with concentrating and paying attention), whereas most boys have **hyperactive-impulsive ADHD** (a form of ADHD that involves being very energized and having trouble sitting still).

Since many girls with ADHD are seen as daydreamers who lack focus and are easily distracted, their subtler symptoms mean that many escape detection by going under the radar. I wasn't diagnosed with ADHD until I was 15. For years my teachers described me as having my head in the clouds. I was called "a daydreamer," "spacey," "lazy" and "unmotivated," when I was none of these things. I actually had ADHD. Since being diagnosed, I've stopped getting frustrated and disappointed in myself. Now that I know I have ADHD, I've been able to put strategies in place to help me manage my symptoms.

Common Signs of ADHD in Girls

Some of the most common signs of ADHD in girls are:

- having difficulty concentrating and maintaining focus

- getting easily distracted

- daydreaming and frequently finding yourself in your own little world

- having difficulty shifting focus from one activity to another

- having difficulty completing tasks, such as finishing homework

- frequently making careless mistakes

- having poor time management

- appearing shy and withdrawn

- getting easily upset and frequently crying

- being disorganized and messy

- being forgetful.

If you have some of these symptoms, you may want to be assessed for ADHD by an experienced professional. Although it may not be the solution for everyone, I've found that ADHD medication has really helped me to be able to concentrate and focus. I used to have to re-read a page several times, because I would lose focus and wasn't able to retain the information. It took forever to do my homework. My ADHD medication has made a world of difference. I can now study so much more efficiently and effectively.

Suggested School Accommodations

Since having ADHD makes it difficult to focus, it can make the classroom environment very challenging. If you have ADHD, there are things that your school and teachers can do to support you and make the classroom environment easier for you. One of the easiest ways to minimize classroom distractions is to ask to be seated in a quiet area, away from the door, window or distracting students. You may also want to explain to your teachers that physical movement helps you to focus and improve your performance. You may want to suggest building short physical activity breaks into your lessons and ask for permission to be allowed to discreetly fidget in a way that doesn't distract other students. For example, allowing you to squeeze a stress ball or play with putty. If you find that you are underperforming on tests and exams, you may want to ask if you can take your tests and exams in a quiet room that has fewer distractions and where you can move around without interrupting other students. The best way to handle any difficulties or challenges caused by your ADHD is by being honest with your teachers and asking for their help and support. It's also important to remember that although ADHD can be a nuisance in the constraints of the classroom environment, many successful people, including famous actors and musicians attribute their success to having ADHD. In the right environment, ADHD can be a superpower.

ANXIETY

Anxiety is very, very common in autistic kids. As you probably already know, it can have a huge impact on your daily life and can make it really tough to cope at school. Although everyone experiences anxiety differently, there are some common triggers that cause us to be anxious at school.

Common Triggers

These include:

- uncertainty and change

- sensory triggers (for example, noisy, crowded, bustling hallways)

- social situations

- expectations, pressures and demands

- anticipating specific situations (for example, having to change for PE class)

- specific fears (for example, being called on in class or being bullied).

Physical Symptoms of Anxiety

Anxiety causes physical symptoms, such as a racing heart rate, feeling short of breath, feeling agitated and distressed, and feeling shaky, sweaty and sick. Anxiety also affects our behavior. Some kids may have meltdowns, outbursts and tantrums, and may become obsessive about routines in order to help them feel more in control. The more anxious I am, the more I rely on the certainty of a schedule or routine. Anxiety becomes a problem when we persistently become overwhelmed by feelings of fear and panic that are beyond our control. Many of us don't like to ask for help. We may struggle in silence throughout the day, only to fall apart as soon as we get home. If you're experiencing high levels of anxiety that are making it difficult for you to cope at school, it's important that your teachers are informed. With your school's support, you can develop strategies that work for you.

Suggested School Accommodations

Accommodations that may help to reduce your anxiety at school include the following:

- Not being required to read aloud or work at the board in front of your class.

- Being assigned a classroom seat near the door, near the front of the room or near the teacher's desk.

- Being assigned a seat near the back of the room in school assemblies.

- Allowing you to identify one teacher or trusted school staff member to seek help from when you are feeling anxious.

- Instead of being made to give a presentation in front of the whole class, being given the option to give the presentation only in front of the teacher.

- Being allowed to take tests and exams in a separate, quiet environment that will help to reduce performance pressure and distractions.

- Being given a "time out" card that allows you to take a break from the classroom. Examples of "time out" activities could include being allowed to walk down the hallway, getting some water, standing outside the classroom door for a few minutes or being allowed to use a mindfulness app with headphones.

- Being paired with a friend who can assist you with transitions during unstructured school breaks, such as during lunch break.

- Being grouped with an adult or student you know well for any field trips.

- Being helped to settle back into school after being absent due to illness—for example, by giving you copies of class notes from lessons you missed.

By putting a support plan in place, you will learn to better manage your symptoms of anxiety throughout the day.

DYSLEXIA

Dyslexia is a specific learning difference that affects the ability to read. Dyslexic kids have difficulties reading fluently and accurately. They may also have difficulties with reading comprehension, spelling and writing. Dyslexia affects everyone differently and can vary in severity. Struggling to decode words is a key sign of dyslexia. Decoding words is the ability to match letters to the corresponding sounds and then to use this skill to read words accurately and fluently.

I wasn't diagnosed with dyslexia until I was ten. The signs were all there. I wrote my letters and numbers the wrong way around, skipped words when reading aloud and misspelled commonly used words. But since I could read, my teachers insisted that I couldn't be dyslexic. Instead, I was labeled "lazy" and "careless." These teachers were wrong. It took a wonderful English teacher to realize that my spelling and reading problems could be dyslexia.

Common Signs of Dyslexia

You may be dyslexic if you:

- often skip over words when reading aloud

- make lots of spelling errors, including misspelling relatively easy words

- regularly write letters and figures the wrong way around (such as writing "6" instead of "9" or "b" instead of "d")

- have to frequently re-read sentences and passages

- read and write at a lower academic level than you speak

- have difficulty planning and writing essays, letters or reports
- have difficulty organizing your written work and have trouble expressing your knowledge in writing
- try to avoid reading and writing whenever possible
- have difficulty taking notes or accurately copying information from the board.

It's important to keep in mind that dyslexia is a condition that affects learning. It does *not* affect intelligence. Dyslexic kids are just as smart as their classmates. In fact, many people view dyslexia as a gift. Dyslexic people are known for being creative, imaginative, innovative and skilled at thinking outside the box. Many people who have struggled with dyslexia have gone on to have successful careers. It is estimated that up to 35% of entrepreneurs in the United States and over 50% of NASA (North American Space Administration) scientists are dyslexic. If you have some of the signs of dyslexia listed above, you may want to have a dyslexia assessment by an experienced professional.

Suggested School Accommodations

Being diagnosed with dyslexia finally made it possible for me to get support in areas I found particularly challenging. Below are some accommodations you may want to request that could make your school day easier for you. You may want to ask that:

- you are not required to read aloud in class

- you aren't penalized for spelling (instead, ask if you can be provided with a separate grade for content and for spelling)

- you can be given oral directions or simplified written directions

- you are provided with an outline of class lectures or copy of class notes

- your teachers avoid allowing students to grade each other's work or tests (I've had this happen and so know how mortifying this can be)

- your teachers minimize the amount of copying from the board (we often copy things from the board incorrectly)

- your teacher provides you with a hard copy of any homework assignments.

Depending on the severity of your dyslexia, you may qualify for extra time on your exams.

DYSPRAXIA

Although autistic kids are known for being clumsy, if your motor skills are significantly affected, you may also be given a formal diagnosis of **dyspraxia**. Dyspraxia (also known as developmental coordination disorder (**DCD**) or motor coordination disorder) is a neurodevelopmental disorder that causes difficulties with coordination and motor skills. It affects fine and gross motor skills and motor planning (the ability to plan and carry out movements and tasks in the right order).

I was diagnosed with dyspraxia when I was eight. I was forever dropping things and bumping into things. I was known for being hopelessly klutzy and clumsy. I've lost count of how many times I've been accused of being a "bull in a china shop." I was also always tripping and falling. I somehow managed to fall up flights of stairs, as well as downstairs. I also struggled to do things most of my classmates could do effortlessly—for example, using scissors, coloring inside the lines, brushing my teeth and getting dressed.

Common Signs of Dyspraxia

You may be dyspraxic if you:

- struggle to maintain your balance

- trip and fall more often than your classmates

- often bump into people and things

- find it difficult to learn new movements in PE class, especially sports that involve balance and require good hand–eye coordination

- take a long time to write, have difficulty gripping a pencil or pen and have really bad handwriting

- struggle to line up columns when doing math problems

- have difficulty cutting your food

- find it especially hard to open the latch on a locker or use a combination lock.

About 50% of students who are autistic or have ADHD also have dyspraxia. If you have some of the signs of dyspraxia listed above, you may want to have a dyspraxia assessment. Although there is no cure for dyspraxia, occupational therapy and physical therapy can be very helpful. Occupational therapists focus on improving coordination, whereas physical therapists work on improving muscle strength. Occupational therapy helped me to learn how to run and ride a bike (something I thought I would never be able to do).

Suggested School Accommodations

Since dyspraxia causes difficulty with activities requiring coordination, you may find that it negatively affects the speed and legibility of your handwriting. Many dyspraxic kids are encouraged to learn how to touch-type so that they can switch to using a laptop at school. I highly recommend transitioning from handwriting to typing. It takes time and commitment to develop your typing skills, but it's well worth the investment. Being able to use a laptop at school has been a massive help to me. If you're dyspraxic, don't let it hold you back. With hard work, dedication and perseverance, you will achieve any goals you set for yourself.

HYPERMOBILITY

It is very common for autistic kids to have hypermobility. I was diagnosed as being hypermobile when I was eight. Hypermobility means that you can move some or all of your joints more than most people can. Some people refer to this as being double-jointed. I have very flexible fingers, wrists, elbows and knees. If you have more than one overly flexible joint, you will be diagnosed with generalized joint hypermobility. Having a wide range of movement can be advantageous. Lots of musicians, dancers and athletes are hypermobile—especially ballerinas and gymnasts. However, hypermobility can also have its disadvantages. People with hypermobile joints can have aches and pains when doing everyday tasks. I frequently have ankle pain and backaches.

Symptoms of Hypermobility

If you have some of the symptoms below, you may be hypermobile:

- muscle aches and pains
- joint aches and pains
- joint stiffness
- foot and ankle pain
- frequent ankle twists and strains
- neck pain
- backaches
- frequent partly or fully dislocated joints.

If you think you may be hypermobile, ask your parents to arrange to have you assessed by a physiotherapist. The assessment is painless and straightforward.

Hypermobility Treatments

Hypermobility can't be cured. Your body's joints are just more flexible than those of other people. However, there are ways to manage your symptoms through a combination of physiotherapy and exercise. I've had physiotherapy that involved doing gentle exercises designed to strengthen and condition the muscles that support my joints. In order to benefit from this approach, it's important to do these exercises on a regular basis. I'll admit that this can be boring and tedious, but it can really help to improve your symptoms. If I'm having a particularly achy day, I'll also take some ibuprofen.

Managing Your Hypermobility

The best way to manage your hypermobility is to do gentle sports that put less stress on your joints. One of the best exercises for hypermobility is swimming. I also tried the Alexander Technique, which focuses on controlled strengthening and posture exercises. If you have hypermobile feet, you may benefit from getting customized insoles for your shoes. The insoles help to realign your foot so that your body weight is more evenly distributed. My insoles really help to reduce my foot, ankle, hip and lower-back pain.

Suggested School Accommodations

If you have hypermobile fingers and hands, handwriting can be very painful. The speed and quality of your handwriting is also likely to be affected. The best way to avoid the discomfort and pain that handwriting causes is to switch to using a laptop. Typing puts a lot less pressure on your finger joints and your wrists. Since I switched from handwriting to typing, I've had a lot less pain and I've found that I'm able to type more and faster than writing by hand.

GASTROINTESTINAL DISORDERS

Gastrointestinal (GI) disorders are very common in autistic kids. The most common GI symptoms include constipation, abdominal pain and diarrhea. Having GI problems at school can be awkward and very stressful.

Suggested School Accommodations

The best way to manage a GI disorder at school is to ask your school to give you a "nurse's pass" which allows you to go to the bathroom or nurse's office without having to interrupt a lesson to ask permission from your teacher. You may also want to ask if your school would be willing to give you permission to use the staff toilets instead of the communal student toilets, which you may be too self-conscious to want to use.

15

Navigating the Perils of Social Media and the Internet

Social media is a big part of being a teen. It plays a significant role in forming our identity. Many of us live our lives online and in the public eye. We share photos on Instagram, live-Tweet our thoughts on Twitter and have our own YouTube channels. Sometimes we don't make the wisest choices about what we're posting, sharing and texting, especially since it's very easy to overstep boundaries without thinking of the consequences.

Navigating the perils of social media can be treacherous for anyone, but autistic teen girls are especially vulnerable. We tend to be trusting and believing. We take people at their word. Our unguarded and unsuspecting nature means that it's easy for others to take advantage of us. Unfortunately, there are people on social media who aren't who they claim to be and who may not have good intentions. Since it's so easy to be deceived and exploited, it's especially important that we always remember to be guarded, wary and suspicious when interacting with people we don't know on social media.

BEING SMART AND SAFE ONLINE

The most important thing to remember when you're online is that it's a public forum. Everyone can read whatever you post. You should never post anything online that you wouldn't want everyone to know. If you post something offensive online, you could find yourself in trouble with your classmates, friends and family, your school and even the police. It can also affect your future, including your university and career opportunities later in life. Universities and future employers frequently check the online profiles of their applicants. This is why it's really important that you understand that the cyber world is the real world, with very real consequences. Below are some rules that will help to ensure that you are being smart and safe online.

Protect Your Identity

The first thing to do is check your privacy settings. Make sure you know what information you're showing to the general public. You can change your privacy setting with just one click of your mouse so only your friends can see your information. When you're on any type of public forum, try to remain as anonymous as possible. Keep *all* private information private, especially information that could help someone determine your actual identity. It's important that you don't share identifying information with people that you don't know in person. The same applies for identifying information about your family and friends. Never reveal anything about other people that could possibly get them into trouble. Private information that you should never allow the public to see includes:

- your full name or the names of your family members
- your home or school address or the address of any of your family or friends
- any type of photograph
- your current location (some phones have automatic GPS apps built in that you may need to turn off)
- phone numbers
- passwords
- credit card numbers.

If someone is asking you to provide this information online, it's a red flag that they may be up to no good. Always check with a parent or trustworthy adult if you're unsure, especially when shopping online or signing up for a website or app.

Use a Gender-Neutral Screen Name

When you create an email address or screen name, use a combination of letters and numbers in both that don't indicate whether you're female. When messaging or using video apps, use a nickname that's different from your screen name. That way, if you ever find yourself in a conversation that makes you uncomfortable, you can exit without having to worry that someone can use your screen name to track you down through your email. Some people who hang out with their friends online set up private groups where only they and the people they invite can interact.

Don't Share Your Passwords

Never share your passwords with anyone, even with your friends. It's hard to imagine, but friendships change. I made the mistake of sharing my passwords with someone I thought was my friend. He actually turned out to be a bully who accessed my iCloud account and circulated some unflattering photos of me (photos of when I wore Harry Potter glasses and had braces). He also sent emails from my account, pretending to be me. It was a tough lesson to learn and one I won't forget. I don't want the same thing to happen to you, so it's better to be safe than sorry. Keep your password private and make sure that you have a strong password. The strongest passwords are made up of a combination of letters and numbers, and don't include names or other identifiable information that can be easily guessed. One trick you might want to try is creating a sentence that means something to you that you can convert into a password. For example, "my dog Rico was born in 2015" creates the password "mdRwbi2015."

Be Nice Online

A great rule to live by is to treat people the way you'd like to be treated. Just because you are online doesn't mean you should act differently from how you would in person. You're probably a really nice person in real life, so be nice online too. Unfortunately, some teens indulge in rude, hateful or threatening behavior online. People who are nasty and aggressive online are at greater risk of being bullied or harassed themselves. If someone's mean to you, try not to react, and definitely don't retaliate. Talk to a trusted adult or a friend who can help.

Think Before You Post

Before you post anything, check your mood! Are you feeling angry or upset? If you are, this isn't the time to be messaging or posting on a social media site. We don't always make good decisions or think straight when we're emotional. Posting personal information or inappropriate messages online can put you at risk from strangers. Before you post something you may regret, step away and do something else instead.

The Internet can be a great place to find people you can really relate to, and it can be easier to socialize and connect online!

...

...

...

But there are always risks to being online.

If you get bullied online, it can be harder to feel like you can escape it.

And you also can't always tell what people's intentions are online, even if they seem nice.

Don't be suspicious of your online friends, but be careful.

Even if someone is making you feel uncomfortable or upset, it can be hard to get away, especially if you're feeling like it's hard to make friends elsewhere.

But it's always okay to step away from anyone who is making you feel unhappy or uncomfortable, no matter what they say or what the situation is.

Remember that the online world isn't the only world in your life, and you can leave any time you like if you feel unsafe there.

EXIT

Don't Post Anything Inappropriate

Be very careful about what you post online. Think about whether the words you've written or the photos you're about to share are ones that you would want other people reading or seeing. A good rule is that if you wouldn't want your grandmother to read it or see it, you probably shouldn't send it or post it. You should absolutely stay away from posting any photos online that show nudity in any form, intimate behavior, illegal behavior, rude or racist behavior or anything that may be deemed inappropriate. You may think that only posting one or a handful of images won't come back to haunt you. But even one image can stay on the Internet forever. Remember that any text messages or photos that you send can be copied and forwarded as soon as you send them, which means that anyone can see them and use them.

Always Remember that the Internet is Forever

Never, ever forget that once you post a comment, text or photo, it can't be undone. Just because the Internet is colossal, it doesn't mean that embarrassing or risqué photos and rude or mean comments will disappear forever. Think about what you post. Sharing provocative photos or intimate details online, even in private emails, could cause you problems in the future. Even people you consider friends can use this information against you, especially if you fall out with each other and they become ex-friends. I suggest that before you post anything, you ask yourself the following questions:

- Would you be okay if your parents, grandparents and teachers saw what you are about to post?

- Would you be okay if a college admissions officer or future employer saw what you are about to post?

If you have any doubt, don't post it. It's always best to err on the side of caution. Be really careful about what you post about yourself or others, and what you allow your friends to post about you, because you may have to live with it for a long, long time.

Don't Respond to Mean Messages

Never respond to an email, text message or online post that is hostile, belligerent and inappropriate or makes you feel uncomfortable in any way. Remember that it isn't your fault if you get a message that is mean or upsets you. If you get an upsetting message, show it to your parents or a trusted adult to see if there is anything you can do to make it stop. Responding to the message is not a good idea, because it may encourage the person and make the situation worse.

Don't Meet Online Friends in Real Life

Don't agree to meet someone in person whom you met online. It's not safe. You can never know for certain that someone you met online is really who they say they are. It could be that the person you are friends with created a fake profile. The person could actually be an adult who is pretending to be a teen.

If you decide that you want to meet someone you met on the Internet, discuss it with your parents and never go to the meeting by yourself. Take a chaperone. Whether you take a friend or a parent, meet in a public place, such as a shopping center or a coffee shop that you're familiar with. The safest thing to do is to have your parents talk with the parents of the other person and for both of you to bring your parents along to the first meeting.

Never Forget the Many Dangers of Sexting

Sexting is when someone shares sexual, naked or semi-naked photos, images or videos of themselves or others, or sends sexually explicit messages. If I can give you one piece of advice, it's to *NEVER* sext. I know that it seems like everyone is sending nudes or "sexy pics," and it can sometimes feel as if the right thing to do is to join in, especially since many teens believe that sexting is a normal way to interact with their friends and classmates. It has become so common that many teens don't see anything wrong with sexting. Talking about sex or sharing nudes online may sound like fun and seem harmless, but it can be very dangerous. It is also illegal.

Below are five reasons why sexting is dangerous and can have serious consequences:

1. **Sexting is considered child pornography, which is a crime.** Creating, sharing or possessing indecent images of anyone under the age of 18 is illegal in the UK and in some states in the US, even if the person doing so is a child and even if the images were created with the permission of the young person. Although the laws on sexting vary from country to country, in many countries exchanging nudes of minors is considered child pornography, which is a crime. You could be breaking the law if you:

   - take a naked photo or video of yourself or of a friend

   - share the naked photo or video of a young person, even if you share it with your friends or classmates who are the same age as you

   - possess, download or store a naked image or video of a young person, even if you have the person's permission.

   There are teens who have been labeled a sex offender for sending or having nude photos of other teens on their phone. There have been cases where teens were charged with a crime, even though the nude photos were of themselves!

2. **Sexting can lead to sexual bullying.** Once a sext is sent into cyberspace, you lose control over your photo or video and are at the mercy of how other people choose to use it. People can use your images in any way they want. Unfortunately, it's very common for teens to use these images to sexually bully, ridicule and embarrass the person

in the photo. One example of sexual bullying is slut shaming, which is when girls are targeted on social media by bullies or mean girls who post rude or sexually explicit comments about them and their bodies.

3. **Sexting can make you vulnerable to sexual predators.** Although a sext is usually for only one person to see, once you send it, there is no way of controlling who sees the image. Lots of teen girls have discovered that a nude they sent to a boy they were dating was circulated around and sometimes even posted online. Once the photo becomes public, there is no way to control who sees it. People who see the photos may make assumptions about you based on your willingness to take and distribute "sexy pics." A sexual predator could get hold of the photo, making you vulnerable to being sexually exploited by people who claim to be someone they're not.

4. **Sexts never go away.** Many teens mistakenly believe that a photo sent by WhatsApp, text message, email or even Snapchat will only be viewed by the person it was sent to. But these images are now out of your control and can be shared, copied and posted online. Even images shared using Snapchat can be screenshot.

5. **Sexting can ruin your reputation.** Indecent images can ruin a teen's online reputation, especially if university admission staff and future employers access the information years later.

The bottom line is that sexting is a really, really, *really* bad idea. I have heard so many stories of teen girls who have had horrible experiences and deeply regret it. There was a 15-year-old girl at my school who had a crush on a boy and who innocently sent him a nude on Snapchat. He had repeatedly asked her to send him a nude. She really liked him and thought he liked her too. She also thought that Snapchat was safe, because the image would delete itself. Within a few days, the photo had been circulated around school. The boy had sent it to a group of friends, who had sent it on to their friends. Before long, almost everyone at school had seen it. The girl couldn't walk down the hallway without people whispering, giggling and making rude comments about her. She was devastated. Sadly, this story isn't unique. You've probably heard a similar story or know someone who this has happened to. The easiest way to prevent this from happening to you is to refrain from sexting. If anyone sends you any nudes or indecent images, delete them.

COMING ACROSS UPSETTING MATERIAL

The Internet is an amazing resource. I use it every day. You probably do too. Although there are countless benefits to using the Internet, there are also risks. One of the dangers of using the Internet is that you can accidentally come across material that you might find upsetting or disgusting. You might have already innocently stumbled across some concerning material, such as violent or scary images, hateful content, sexual material or harmful advice encouraging eating disorders and self-harm. I certainly have. It's normal to feel scared or worried about seeing something upsetting online. If you unintentionally find yourself accessing material you find upsetting, I suggest that you immediately close the site. If you're very upset, speak to an adult who you can confide in about what you've seen. You may want to consider using an Internet safety tool, such as an Internet filter to screen out disturbing content. However, at some point, it's important that you develop the skills you'll need to avoid coming across disturbing content in the future.

MAKING ONLINE PURCHASES

Since I hate going to shopping malls, my parents sometimes let me use their credit card to buy clothes, makeup and shoes online. Having access to an infinite array of items, next-day delivery and great discounts makes shopping online very convenient and appealing. However, always keep in mind that there are lots of online scams and fraudulent websites. If you're starting to shop online, it's important to use reputable shopping sites and to check customer reviews. Read reviews to find out if other people have had a positive or negative experience with the site. When making an online purchase, be alert as to the type of information you are being asked to provide to complete the transaction. Make sure you think it's necessary for the retailer to be asking for this information. It's safest to use a credit card (rather than a debit card) for online purchases, because the credit card company will usually refund you if the item you purchased isn't delivered or isn't what you ordered.

CYBERBULLYING

Cyberbullying is when someone bullies or harasses others using technology. People who bully others online may send offensive text messages, make fun of someone in a chat room or post cruel messages on a person's Facebook or Instagram. They might send intimidating and threatening emails or post unflattering images of someone online. It may be that the cyberbully is a former friend or someone you know, or the cyberbully could be an anonymous person hiding behind a screen name. Many teens have experienced cyberbullying on social media. If you have ever been cyberbullied or are currently being cyberbullied, you're not alone. Below is some advice on what to do if you're being cyberbullied:

- Know that it's not your fault. If someone is repeatedly cruel to you, you mustn't blame yourself. No one deserves to be treated this way.

- Don't reply to cyberbullying messages; it's better to ignore them. The cyberbully might be looking for attention and for a reaction. You also don't want to risk provoking a bully. If you ignore them, you take away their power.

- If you feel comfortable doing so, tell the person to stop.

- The only good news about bullying online or on phones is that it can usually be captured, saved and shown to someone who can help. Save the abusive emails, texts or messages you receive. You may also want to make a note of dates and times you receive bullying messages, as well as details of the cyberbully's username. It may help to have all this information, just in case you need evidence in the future.

- Take advantage of online safety tools. Most social media apps and services allow you to block the person. You can also report the problem to the service providers. If you're getting threats of physical harm, you should call your local police (with a parent or trusted adult's help).

- If you are bullied repeatedly, change your username or profile, and use a screen name that doesn't give away any information about you.

- If ignoring the messages doesn't make the cyberbullying stop, ask for help from an adult, whether a parent, a teacher or another trusted adult.

If someone you know is being cyberbullied, support the person being bullied. If the person is a friend, you can listen and see how to help. If you're not already friends, even a kind word can help them to feel less isolated and alone. At the very least, help the person by not passing along a mean message and by not giving positive attention to the person doing the bullying.

Don't Measure Your Own Life Based on What Others Post

It's easy to get the impression that everyone else's life is perfect. What people post on social media can be really misleading. People typically post happy photos and stories online. They don't usually share their boring or sad moments or their unflattering photos. Don't assume that others have better lives than you do, based on what they post.

It isn't unusual for teen girls to sieve through hundreds of photos, agonizing over which photos to post online. Many teen girls spend hours pruning their online identities in order to project an idealized image of themselves. It's no longer just models in fashion magazines who are photoshopped to look thinner and impossibly beautiful. Most teen girls now alter their images too. It's really easy to use phone apps to filter or alter your images so that you can compete with the photos your classmates are posting. The danger of altering your images to appear thinner or more attractive is that it can lead to a poor body image and a feeling of dissatisfaction with the way you look in real life. It is also really easy to get caught up in how much people like you and your appearance by obsessing over how many "likes" you receive.

It's important to remember that a lot of what teen girls post isn't real. A much better way to value yourself is to feel good about what you can do, instead of how you look and what you own. Find an activity that makes you feel good about yourself and that builds your self-esteem. It could be art or music or sports or reading or learning a foreign language or volunteering—anything that you're interested in that involves developing your talents and switches the focus from what you look like to who you are and what you can accomplish.

A WORD ABOUT SELF-ESTEEM

Our self-esteem—how we value and perceive ourselves—can be very fragile. Self-esteem is based on our opinion and belief about ourselves. It can be hard to think positively of ourselves when we're constantly aware of how "different" we are and we're constantly aware of the fact that we don't quite belong.

Being an autistic girl in a neurotypical world is hard. We're always trying to make sense of the world around us—a world that is often uncertain, disorienting and confusing. We're always trying to decipher what other people are thinking and feeling. We're always trying to fit in, even though we don't feel as if we do. In the past, we may have had difficulties making friends and keeping them. We may have been bullied and socially rejected by our classmates. We have also had to overcome more obstacles and challenges than most of our classmates, such as motor coordination problems, social challenges, anxiety and learning differences (ADHD, dyslexia or dyspraxia). All of these negative experiences and challenges can chip away at our confidence and our sense of self-worth. However, our experiences can also show us what we're made of; they make us stronger and wiser. If you have the strength of character and resilience to overcome all these difficulties, you can accomplish anything you set out to do!

16

Celebrating Neurodiversity

When I told you a bit about myself at the beginning of this book, I mentioned that I'm a neurodiversity advocate. You may be wondering what **neurodiversity** is and why I'm advocating for it. Neurodiversity is based on the idea that each one of us has a brain that is unique, which means that there is no such thing as a "normal" brain. People who are autistic or who have dyslexia, dyspraxia, ADHD and other neurological conditions don't have a faulty or abnormal brain; our brain is simply wired differently compared with the majority of people. Our differently wired brain makes us better at some things and worse at others.

I became a neurodiversity advocate, because I'm passionate about changing people's perceptions about autistic people and people with learning differences— in other words, people who are neurodivergent. In November 2018, I launched **Neurodiversity Celebration Week**, a campaign that aims to encourage schools to recognize the strength and talents of their neurodivergent students. I hope to flip the narrative so that teachers shift from focusing on our weaknesses to also focusing on the things we're good at. I believe that it's time we begin to look at neurodivergent students in a different light. I also believe that it's time we change the negative perceptions and stereotypes that still exist about students who have special educational needs.

The tide is definitely turning. As an autistic teen girl, I have been incredibly inspired by Greta Thunberg, the autistic teen climate change activist whose Fridays For Future movement had inspired millions of people around the world to strike against climate change. I have never been able to identify with someone so closely. Like Greta, I've spent most of my life being out of synch, out of step and out of reach of how to be "normal." So, when an autistic teen girl with ADHD stands up and defies the limitations that are too often placed on us, she paves the way for you and me to start seeing ourselves in a positive light. Greta refers to her autism as a "gift," a "superpower" and the source of her passion, drive, out-of-the-box thinking and ability to cut through rhetoric. In addition to helping to save the planet, Greta is changing people's perceptions of autism and how autistic kids view themselves.

I hope that Neurodiversity Celebration Week will also play a role in helping to change the way neurodivergent students perceive themselves. In May 2018, over 340 schools and colleges and more than 315,000 students in six countries took part in the first-ever Neurodiversity Celebration Week. This is only the beginning. I hope that in the future Neurodiversity Celebration Week will be even bigger and bolder. I hope that thousands of schools and millions of students will take part.

If you'd like to join the neurodiversity movement and help to create a society that is more accepting and understanding of people who are different, please consider encouraging your school to take part in the next Neurodiversity Celebration Week. I'm happy to help in any way I can, so please get in touch at:

siena@neurodiversity-celebration-week.com

My dream is that every school will eventually participate in Neurodiversity Celebration Week so that no other kid is made to feel that they are a failed version of "normal." We're all—each and every one of us—individual and unique. It's time to celebrate this!

Where to Find More Information

AUTISM-RELATED WEBSITES
Ambitious about Autism

www.ambitiousaboutautism.org.uk

Ambitious about Autism is the national charity for children and young people with autism. They provide services, raise awareness and understanding, and campaign for change.

Autistic & Unapologetic

www.autisticandunapologetic.com

An engaging autism awareness site by James Sinclair, who describes himself as a lad on a journey to find out what makes him (autis)tic.

Quantum Leap Mentoring

www.qlmentoring.com

A website I created when I was 13 years old to mentor and support autistic students and students with learning differences. I provide child-friendly information on autism, dyslexia and dyspraxia. I also share the tips and tricks that I use to help me to succeed in school.

Speaking of Autism

www.speakingofautismcom.wordpress.com

A blog by autistic 17-year-old Quincy Hansen from Denver, Colorado. Quincy started the blog to reach a wider audience with an autistic take on autism, neurodiversity and acceptance. He hopes his blog will provide a place for other autistic people to read and relate.

Steph's Two Girls

www.stephstwogirls.co.uk

A fun and uplifting site about family life with two girls, one of whom has a specific type of autism called Pathological Demand Avoidance (PDA).

The National Autistic Society

www.autism.org.uk

The National Autistic Society is a national charity that aims to help transform lives, change attitudes and create a society that works for autistic people.

Understood

www.understood.org

A content-rich website that aims to help autistic children and children with learning differences to unlock their strengths and reach their full potential through the use of state-of-the-art technology, personalized resources, videos, practical tips and much more.

BULLYING WEBSITES

Anti-Bullying Alliance

www.anti-bullyingalliance.org.uk

The Anti-Bullying Alliance is a coalition of organizations and individuals united against bullying. The website contains tools, information and advice on what to do if you're being bullied.

Anti-Bullying Pro

www.antibullyingpro.com

The Diana Award's Anti-Bullying Campaign involves a number of different projects aimed at reducing bullying in schools. One of the main projects is the Anti-Bullying Ambassadors Programme which has trained over 24,000 young people across the United Kingdom to lead anti-bullying campaigns in their schools.

Ditch the Label

www.ditchthelabel.org

Ditch the Label believes in a world that is fair, equal and free from all types of bullying. It seeks to combat bullying by tackling the root issues and by supporting young people who are affected. The website has useful information and advice on different types of bullying.

MENTAL HEALTH WEBSITES

Childline

www.childline.org.uk

Childline is charity that focuses on helping anyone under 19 in the United Kingdom with any issue they're going through. The website has lots of useful information and advice on mental health.

Young Minds

www.youngminds.org.uk

The United Kingdom's leading charity fighting for children and young people's mental health. The website has useful information on how to improve your mental health.

SEXUALITY AND GENDER IDENTITY WEBSITES

BGiOK

www.bgiok.org.uk

Being Gay is Okay is a website that offers information and advice for gay, lesbian, bisexual and unsure youth.

Mermaids

www.mermaidsuk.org.uk

Mermaids is passionate about supporting children, young people and their families to achieve a happier life in the face of adversity. The charity works to raise awareness about gender nonconformity in children and young people.

The Mix

www.themix.org.uk

A leading support service for young people that is there to help you take on any challenge you're facing, including mental health.

Young Stonewall

www.youngstonewall.org.uk

Young Stonewall is focused on letting all young lesbian, gay, bi and trans people (as well as those who are questioning) know they're not alone.

USEFUL WEBSITES

ADHD Foundation

www.adhdfoundation.org.uk

ADHD Foundation is a national charity that aims to improve the emotional wellbeing, educational attainment, behavior and life chances of people with ADHD through a better understanding and self-management of their ADHD and other conditions. The website offers specific advice for young people.

Dyslexia Advantage

www.dyslexicadvantage.org

Dyslexic Advantage promotes the positive identity, community and achievement of dyslexic people by focusing on their strengths. The website has resources, dyslexia articles, learning strategies and tips, and much more.

Dyspraxia Foundation

www.dyspraxiafoundation.org.uk

The Dyspraxia Foundation is a charity that seeks to increase the understanding of dyspraxia. Their website has lots of useful information and tips on how to cope with the challenges of being dyspraxic.

Made By Dyslexia

www.madebydyslexia.org

Made By Dyslexia is a global charity led by successful and famous dyslexics. The charity aims to help the world properly understand and support dyslexia.

Neurodiversity Celebration Week

www.neurodiversity-celebration-week.com

Neurodiversity Celebration Week aims to encourage schools to recognize the strengths and talents of their neurodivergent students. The website lists the schools taking part in Neurodiversity Celebration Week from around the world. It also includes inspiring and uplifting videos, posters and resources designed to support autistic children and children with learning differences.

Smart Kids with Learning Disabilities

www.smartkidswithld.org

Smart Kids with Learning Disabilities seeks to educate, guide and inspire parents of children with learning disabilities or ADHD so that they can help to realize their children's significant gifts and talents.

Recommended Reading

A Smart Girl's Guide: Boys—Surviving Crushes, Staying True to Yourself, and Other Love Stuff by Nancy Holyoke (American Girl Publishing, 2015)

A Smart Girl's Guide: Drama, Rumors, and Secrets—Staying True to Yourself in Changing Times by Nancy Holyoke (American Girl Publishing, 2015)

A Smart Girl's Guide: Friendship Troubles—Dealing with Fights, Being Left Out, and the Whole Popularity Thing by Angela Martini and Patti Kelley Criswell (American Girl Publishing, 2013)

A Smart Girl's Guide: Knowing What to Say—Finding the Words to Fit Any Situation by Patti Kelley Criswell (American Girl Publishing, 2018)

A Smart Girl's Guide—Liking Herself: Even on the Bad Days by Laurie E. Zelinger (American Girl Publishing, 2018)

A Smart Girl's Guide: Manners—The Secret to Grace, Confidence, and Being Your Best by Nancy Holyoke (American Girl Publishing, 2013)

A Smart Girl's Guide to the Internet: How to Connect with Friends, Find What You Need, and Stay Safe Online by Sharon Cindrich (American Girl Publishing, 2009)

A Smart Girl's Guide: Worry—How to Feel Less Stressed and Have More Fun by Judith Woodburn and Nancy Holyoke (American Girl Publishing, 2016)

Aspergirls: Empowering Females with Asperger Syndrome by Rudy Simone (Jessica Kingsley Publishers, 2010)

Camouflage: The Hidden Lives of Autistic Women by Dr. Sarah Bargiela (Jessica Kingsley Publishers, 2019)

Friends: Making Them and Keeping Them by Patti Kelley Criswell (American Girl Publishing, 2015)

Sex, Puberty and All That Stuff: A Guide to Growing Up by Jacqui Bailey (Franklin Watts, 2016)

The Autism-Friendly Guide to Periods by Robyn Steward (Jessica Kingsley Publishers, 2019)

The Care and Keeping of Us: A Sharing Collection for Girls and Their Moms by Dr. Cara Natterson and Emma MacLaren Henke (American Girl Publishing, 2015)

The Care and Keeping of You 2: The Body Book for Older Girls by Dr. Cara Natterson (American Girl Publishing, 2013)

The Feelings Book: The Care and Keeping of Your Emotions by Lynda Madison (American Girl Publishing, 2018)

Your Happiest You: The Care and Keeping of Your Mind and Spirit by Judy Woodburn (American Girl Publishing, 2017)

Index

Index